CUSTOMER SERVICE SAVVY

THE KEY TO YOUR BUSINESS SUCCESS

DEVELOP IT
USE IT
SEE YOUR SUCCESS

CUNNING AND CLEVER THOUGHTS BY
ROBERT E. LEVINSON

Order this book online at www.trafford.com
or email orders@trafford.com

Most Trafford titles are also available at major online book retailers.

Print information available on the last page.

ISBN: 978-1-4907-8347-5 (sc)
ISBN: 978-1-4907-8346-8 (e)

Trafford rev. 07/19/2017

 www.trafford.com
North America & international
toll-free: 1 888 232 4444 (USA & Canada)
fax: 812 355 4082

INTRODUCTION

Customer service costs little or nothing and is easy to incorporate into your company style. It adds money in the till more easily and less expensively than advertising. It makes people feel good – both giver and receiver.

It is up to you to determine if your company meets the highest standards or needs of customer service or to decide whether immediate revisions are needed in this ever-changing, global market. Is another company providing better customer service than you or your company? If you don't have the right priorities in place, there are plenty of companies all over the world waiting to capitalize on any mistakes your company makes.

Does this only apply to the entrepreneur? Of course not! The management team and every single employee that works in any business need to have the same philosophy of good customer service in order for a company to succeed. Every action that is taken—at any level—can help make or break your goals for success.

NOTE FROM THE AUTHOR

This book is about all forms of interpersonal relationships—which we commonly call customer service—whether your company is a doctor's office, retail store, restaurant, law firm, nonprofit organization or any other business. Even if you generally rely on social media, texting or email for basic communication, eventually everything boils down to one human being talking to another human being.

I've noticed that over the years our society has lost the knack of respect, courtesy and understanding of other human beings in day-to-day business, which has an adverse effect not only on business but also your personal satisfaction.

Perhaps you are wondering: What makes me qualified to discuss this subject? I've had a diverse career in many fields of business, in addition to working with nonprofit organizations and academic organizations. In every endeavor, the ability to sparkle in my relationships with others helped my success.

> Want greater success? Learn to sparkle in your relationships with others and show customer savvy that attracts and appeals.

Example: When I was in the manufacturing business making steel building products, I had a meeting with all of my distributors every year for sales and marketing purposes. One year, I hired management consultants who went to those customers to study their operations and determine how the use of my products would earn them the most money possible. When I held the next annual sales meeting, I didn't conduct any of our normal sales business. Rather, I had my consultants show my distributors how they could improve their own business. No one believed that I would spend all that money and time to help my customers become more successful, but I never once promoted my own products in that meeting. This unconventional form of customer service worked well for all parties. Different? Of course. Successful? You bet.

You have customers regardless of the business or field you are in. Throughout my career in all its various fields, I was able to:

1) Personalize every relationship with my customers;
2) Make them feel important;
3) Dedicate myself to helping them make a profit;
4) Make them better known in the community;
5) Help them become more successful businesspeople; and
6) Work with them to achieve success.

Example: When working in the candle business, I sold candles all over the United States. Every year we mailed two bayberry candles as a holiday scent to potential customers and marketed them as a holiday gift item that they could send their customers as a gift. We were always very generous in giving away samples of our products, which in turn helped us to be successful.

My father, brother and I had a manufacturing business which we sold to American Standard, Inc. after my father died in 1969. American Standard was a large publicly traded company, and I became vice president of one of the nine divisions. When I walked into my first meeting with the big shots, I was shivering in my shoes, but I was full of questions. Apparently, the other VPs had no chutzpah, because they later turned to me to ask the questions they needed answered!

When my wife and I vacationed in Fort Lauderdale, Florida, we played on a golf course next to a 50-room hotel. One day, there was a guy behind pushing us to hurry during our game. When we got back to the starter, I asked who he was—turns out he owned the golf course! I thought to myself, "Maybe we can just buy him and the hotel out. We ought to buy this place." Then we went to the hotel, met the owner, had a couple martinis and started to negotiate the buyout of the hotel and golf course.

We didn't get that one, but by then I was in the mood to go into the hotel business, so eventually I bought a different hotel. Shortly after that, I was at a party in Fort Lauderdale and met someone selling land, so I went ahead and bought land for another hotel. After ten years I left American Standard, but by then I had already decided to stay in the hotel business and ended up owning three hotels.

Throughout my career, I have written articles and books about business skills, customer savvy, finding success, never retiring and even finding love in your "golden years." Recently I moved into an independent retirement community where I met a young man working in one of the departments whom I felt had the potential for great success. I gave him one of my previous business books, and ever since he read it he has constantly been telling me that his success in promotions has been in part due to the lessons he learned from my book.

I intend this book to be a wake-up call for people. We need to stress the value of good customer service.

Good customer service promotes strong relationships and complements sound business strategies.

The best part is that you don't have to invest any money in it—providing good customer service costs you nothing and guarantees success.

Where else can you find a business tool that doesn't cost anything, but can be an easy road to success?

The key ingredient for success: Good customer service is established by the person in charge. It starts at the top.

The leaders of any organization set the integrity, policy, atmosphere and personality of the organization, and whatever they choose and do will permeate the entire organization. You have to fire up your employees and stimulate your associates. It can be relentless, difficult and maybe even complicated to implement and maintain, but customer service works.

I finally stopped working a day job at age 90, so I have had 70 years of experience building leadership skills. I've learned that people don't change, so the experiences and advice in this book are as true today as they were 70 years ago—and will still be true in 70 more years. You do not need a PhD to follow these ideas. Take the mystery out of the techniques for success.

Be successful in relationships and you will be successful in business.

CONTENTS

BETTER CUSTOMER SERVICE: CHALLENGE AND OPPORTUNITY

- Does your company have clear-cut, stated company policies advocating good customer service?
- Is your management team passionate about customer service?
- Do you empower your team to make important decisions?
- Do you trust and allow them to handle issues?
- Do you provide them with the support they might need to do their job well?
- What do you think any member of your team would do if they needed to make an important decision?

As you review these questions, you should be able to clearly evaluate the way you run your business or how you work as a representative of your company both by the answers that quickly come to mind, but also those that you find yourself second-guessing.

If you are an entrepreneur, think about your management team and all the employees you rely on to keep your business running. Your efforts can make or break the difference on whether you can hold on to your business, keep your position, move further up or even one day reach higher goals for yourself and your company.

Some of the important questions you should review below may not relate to the position you hold, but your interpretation of your responsibilities and ethics for the company that you work for will still make or break your personal career, as well as affect the company you're currently with:

1) When was the last time you picked up the phone and called a customer or emailed them to see how satisfied they are with your company's product or service?
2) When was the last time you listened to a customer complaint, either on the phone, face-to-face or electronically?
3) Can you recall the last time that you were introduced to a customer?
4) Have you ever sat down with any new employees and emphasized your company's strong personal policy on professional customer service?

It is crucial for any business to have the fewest negative business encounters as possible in order to succeed. Small, simple favors and courtesies impress customers with your company's credibility, and this enhances their loyalty.

Example:
Customer: I hate to bring this up but… When I was in here the other day, the small $7.50 item on this receipt was not included in my package.

Employee: You should have come back immediately! When did you say that was?

Customer: It was last Tuesday, or maybe -

Employee: (interrupting) Well, I'm sorry, but the receipt is dated Wednesday.

Customer: It doesn't matter what day it was or if I get my money back. It's not a big deal. However, I never expected that you would embarrass me like this or I wouldn't have said anything. I'll pay more attention when I shop here—or I'll simply go somewhere else. It's certainly not my fault that you made a mistake.

Result: An unhappy customer walks away from your company because of the poor judgment shown by your employee.

Example:

Customer: I ordered a thermometer from your company, Sharper Image, and I've had it for a few weeks, but it does not work.

Employee: Do you have the receipt?

Customer: No.

Employee: Do you remember when you bought it?

Customer: No.

Employee: Well, let me look up your name in our system…

(Few minutes wait)

Employee: I can see that you bought it under a year ago. We are sending you a new thermometer immediately, and thank you very much for your patience.

Result: This customer's loyalty to your company was just enhanced by the integrity of your employee.

Customers are entitled to receive the most professional customer service from the companies who receive their hard-earned money for the things they purchase—from shoes and hamburgers to professional services and hotel rooms… but often they don't.

If customers don't receive this level of commitment from your company, trust me, there will be a competitor just waiting to capitalize on it.

The Decline in Customer Service

You and I know that highly professional service to customers does not always prevail. Personally, I've reached the point where I'm surprised when I find good service. I've had friends tell me that they no longer receive special attention or even common courtesy when they take their cars in to be serviced, or deal with store employees, government workers, physicians' offices or medical facilities.

An all-too-prevalent attitude seems to be that—the customer, client, patient, guest or whatever—is an inconvenience, a necessary evil that should be dealt with as perfunctorily as possible.

This is a shame for both seller and buyer, but it provides an opportunity for any companies that prioritize service to take the market.

From the seller's point of view, good service is the best and easiest way to build a successful, growing business. It's a way to create a strong business for the long haul. For the buyer, it adds to the ease of shopping and their ability to enjoy spending the money they've worked hard to earn.

Poor service, on the other hand, leads to aggravation and disgust. Throughout my career as the owner of a manufacturing firm, as a corporate executive in a successful company and as the owner of three hotels in Florida, I've always stressed customer service. It is my way of life in my career, and I have passed it along to my associates. It works! It is in everyone's own self-interest to emphasize the highest level of service. This is what makes it so hard for me to understand why so many companies fail to practice this simple technique or allow their policies on it to slowly disintegrate.

Nevertheless, the truth is that many customers are getting shortchanged. They are paying for a service, and no matter what amount of money they spend, large or small, if they are not receiving it, I literally consider this a crime: stealing.

How to Turn Things Around

It's important for organizations to talk about customer service. Come up with ideas to improve customer service. Try to think outside the box about how you can be different from the rest. It is so rewarding when you have an interaction that leads to continued success with a customer or colleague. How many times do we hear: "I love to shop here because they're always so helpful." "I love my doctor, and his staff is wonderful." "I love my lawyer because even when he's out of town his staff will bend over backwards." "I love shopping at Publix because they're always asking to help me." "I HATE going to this place. Maybe I have to go because I can't get this product anywhere else conveniently, but they're always so gloomy."

The atmosphere of customer service is a stimulant for success. It's no secret, and yet so many organizations fail to give it thought. Why aren't we knocking ourselves out with this free and guaranteed technique for success?

One thing that can actually help you with customer service is watching your competition. Today's organizations realize that they face the implications of competition, both from within the United States and from other countries, but few are able to escape its wrath. How do you make sure, no matter what level you're at, that your company stays ahead of all the other competitors?

- Better goods and services
- Better locations
- Better salespeople
- Better sales policies
- Better business management
- Better customer service

These are the elements that our competitors are going to be examining and that you must deal with on a daily basis in your own organization. This is especially important. All of these factors come into play when it comes to winning over and building a good relationship with a customer, and taking a look at how the competition is doing will help you improve your own policies.

If we ignore our competitors, we are playing Russian Roulette. Never underestimate the hidden power of the competition! Even if your competitors have mediocre sales policies and salespeople, there will be other elements of their business that are strong and must be overcome for you to win the game. Think about what can happen to companies who do not research competitor information.

The easiest way to have information on your competitors collected is on the "Street"—by utilizing every level of employee in your organization. You must have a process in place for every employee to be able to share their thoughts and their observations with the highest level decision makers of your company. Many times studies are done by the company executives, but they're not working with information that is accurate or reliable enough—make sure that's not your company!

In some cases, collected competitor information obtained from customers may be incorrect or contain misleading data. Generally, not many customers will reply. Without enough input, how can you process an objective overview from your customer base? That is why the input from every level of employee in your organization should be considered valuable.

Good, reliable information is necessary in order to assess your position relative to your competition.

A Golden Opportunity

Look at your competition. How are they selling their products and services? Making yourself more aware of what the market is doing will motivate you to play up your strongest features. As the 1944 Johnny Mercer song says, "Accentuate the Positive." Always play up your strongest features when speaking to a potential customer.

Example: All of us take for granted the ease of ordering a pizza and having it delivered to our doorsteps, but it wasn't always that way. Years ago, a privately-owned local pizza operator in California experienced a 30% drop in business because a national chain opened up in his market. In order to fight it, he came up with an idea to organize the independent operators into a home delivery network. It had already worked for independent florists when a company called FTD created home delivery of flowers nationwide. It was a terrific move on his part and showed great imagination in fighting the competition. He found a niche that he was able to develop into a successful sales and marketing idea. Today, individual restaurants have finally realized they face the same problem because of their own lack of home delivery. Enter Delivery Dudes, a national still-growing company that has created their own niche to solve this problem. Contracting with local restaurants in different areas, their delivery service continues to grow, despite the high cost they charge. This shows how important good customer service is. It can make or break your company.

Example: In 1893, Charles Cretors developed a commercial way to pop corn. When I was young, the main way to have popcorn at home was to buy raw corn and use a "popper," a special device that would pop the corn. Suddenly, Cretors had a competitor. After that, the development of microwave ovens created another new type of competition: "microwavable popcorn." All three companies are still viable, but each has a different use and market—the commercial popper is used at fairs and movie theaters; the popper and the microwavable popcorn can both be used at home, but each one has a distinct market because people will choose one over the other because of their different lifestyles. This shows the value of paying attention to your competition and analyzing the SWOT (Business Analysis Model: Strengths, Weaknesses, Opportunities, Threats) of your specific product.

Example: One of the clearer examples of a company staying up with the competition is the manufacturer of Arm & Hammer Baking Soda. This product was destined to become useless with the development of new foods and mixes. So, what did the manufacturer do? It came up with and marketed the many new uses of the product, such as keeping the refrigerator odor free and using it in the laundry. Still in use today? Of course.

Competition can similarly inspire the development of new products and ideas, but there are times these ideas or products can make existing products obsolete. That was the boat that carbon paper manufacturers found themselves in; technology changed their industry and virtually eliminated the use of their product. Still in use today? You might not even know what or how it was used.

New technology does this to many products almost overnight. Companies that keep up with the technology of their industry are the ones that stay on top. This means that getting competitive information is not just obtaining prices, but:

- What R&D is the competition doing?
- What is the competition doing to make the product or service better, more convenient or more versatile?

New materials and their applications, and new equipment to more efficiently and productively manufacture products are all important elements in the competitive race. Most successful companies are never satisfied, because they realize that their product cannot stay the same forever. They are constantly changing and, in general, keeping up with technology.

There can be exceptions to this rule—for instance, Ritz Crackers. They have never changed their original product. Although they have added additional Ritz Crackers with cheese and other mixture fillings, you can still buy the original!

Look what happened to Coca Cola. Whether by accident or by a carefully planned program, their attempt to change their recipe became an international event—it was one of the greatest promotions of all times. However, as we know, Coke had to keep the original—it's a "Classic."

How Your Competition Can Help You

As mentioned, one fundamental aspect of developing good customer service is to study your competition very carefully:

- Pick out areas where your competitors are weak
- Develop these particular areas into your own strengths
- Push and promote these ideas to your customers
- Sharpen your edge
- Develop exciting new products and new sales

Example: Next door to one of my hotels was a well-known competitor. They were totally inadequate in planning meetings and did a very bad job with their banquet food operation. We knew this and capitalized on it by encouraging potential banquet customers to visit our competitor and compare the way they planned a meeting with the way we handled it. Much of our business came to us because the competitor was inadequate. Yet, we could not assume that this would always be the case—we had to constantly monitor the competitor's operation for changes.

Example: Having minor car repairs made is often a problem for people. The car dealership may be costly and far from your home. You may have to make an appointment and reserve time to get there, which can be inconvenient. It's easier to take your car to a local service station for repairs, so in the past, both Standard Oil of Ohio and Shell developed programs to capitalize on this problem by including auto repair shops in their service stations. It gave the stations more volume potential and provided a great service to customers. Evaluating their competition became the driving force behind developing another idea to sell still more gas and oil. As time went on, attached service stations became costly and inefficient and are not common. Remaining fluid in an ever-changing marketplace is as essential as evaluating your competition for ways to create new opportunities. Today, Tesla dealers bring their customers back by offering free electric charging and a car that never needs to be taken to a dealer. Of course, the luxury marketplace is different from the lower end, but if Tesla had not been aware of their market, they could not have established their place in it as well as they did.

Example: "Convenience stores" are often successful throughout the United States because they provide a place that is always open, handy and convenient. They fulfill a customer need and provide a service. More recently, convenience stores have developed "mini-restaurant" areas in their stores where customers not only buy the food, but eat it on the premises. (Interestingly, many gas stations have added convenience stores as a more cost-effective way to make money than the service station was in the past.) Most grocery chains were not too worried, but some decided to stay open 24/7. The idea was that in offering a full line of products, they could cut into the competition from the convenience store business. The additional costs were not too great, and they were able to add volume business by doing this. The all-night grocery idea enabled people to plan their full shopping needs around their own schedules and not the store's. Now when they needed something fast, customers could visit their regular store where a wider selection of products was available to them. "Impulse buying" meant customers probably bought more on each visit simply because they were in a full-service store. Grocery chains have developed more ideas for meeting the competition such as: preparing already cooked foods and "take-out" salad bars, along with a complete delicatessen counter.

Competition continues to drive the food industry segment in many new directions, and it is really jumping! Each competitor is striving for a larger amount of the food dollar and is changing peoples' eating habits to accomplish this goal.

The same is true in other industries.

Example: Just look how the floral industry is changing. For over 70 years, grocery stores sold "non-food items," mostly using rack-jobbers who fill the racks, service the store daily and maintain inventory. Flowers are one of those non-food products that have grown into a major department in many grocery stores and convenience stores. Grocery stores have honed in on the market serviced by small, local florists, who are now again facing additional competition with the ability to order flowers online efficiently and easily, bypassing them completely. Each flower provider has a specific market, from Baby Boomers to Generation Z, and each needs to continually monitor their competition and their own market plan as the market continues to change.

Knowing What the Competition is Doing

In my organization, we kept an eye on how our competitors answered their telephones and followed-up inquiries. Usually, they were very bad, to their detriment, but to our advantage. We implemented a strong customer service policy, with a fetish about answering letters, inquiries, and the telephone.

- Give customers respect!
- Give them attention!
- Give them what will satisfy their needs!
- Adjust your service to them!

Customers will at the very least feel your concern when you respond quickly, and once you secure a customer's loyalty, knock yourself out to keep it. You can go a long way simply by NOT making the same mistakes your competition is making.

It's amazing to see how badly most companies deal with customers on the phone or answering letters.

Example: I once wrote a letter to the General Managers of various hotels around the country, informing them that one of my good customers (an international giant corporation) was traveling to their city and was seeking a special price on rooms. Would you believe it took several weeks before some of the managers answered my letter? Others didn't even bother to reply.

Example: A CEO once told me how concerned he was with his company's service, so he had various people call his company and, for example, count the rings on the phone and report it to him. It was a way for him to get a reading on how fast his people responded to a customer. Clever? You bet.

Remember:

- Make sure your management team knows what your competition is doing: their pricing structure, their financial policies and their methods of doing business.
- Use the weaknesses of the competition to develop your policies.
- Take full advantage of these weaknesses, but watch them carefully because they may change. You must be able and willing to make changes in your own policies in response to theirs.
- Discuss these subjects in detail with your staff.

Should You "Knock" the Competition?

Never try selling a product or service by "talking down" a competitor; simply know the competition's weaknesses. This enables you to develop your pluses around these points. Know all about your competitor, and point out to customers the features of your company that are superior to the competition. Also, try the pie trick.

What's that? One day, I had a potential customer in one of our hotel restaurants. I explained how we lived up to what we promised our customers. When it came time for dessert, I asked my guest if he would like to try a piece of "real" Key Lime pie. In Florida, this is a specialty; many places have imitation Key Lime, which is green. He agreed to try it, and when he took the first bite, he blurted out, "Boy! That is absolutely the real thing!" I, of course, sat back with a big smile and said, "I told you what our company does. We mean what we say." Obviously, this made my point and fortified our sales presentation to him. Find the appropriate pie trick for your industry.

Checkpoint Quiz:

- What are my competitors' weaknesses?
- How can I use them as a guide to develop and improve my organization's policy?
- How do I make a customer's experience with us worth talking about?

SAVVY PRODUCT DEVELOPMENT

In every aspect of the business world, competition is an unavoidable and significant force that should drive the development of your strategies for new products or services, as well as the subsequent marketing, selling and customer service.

Organizations must carefully analyze their market plan after determining how to build the "better mousetrap." From a psychological point of view, we can either be inspired by competition or impaired by the lack of it. Obviously, competition and product development are closely related. We should be asking ourselves:

- Has it been done before?
- Can I do a better job in providing a product or service?
- Is it a new idea?
- Can I solve a problem in a new way with a new product?

How New Products Create New Needs

The idea process and study of new products should be systematic, falling into two general categories:

1. A completely new idea for something that has never been produced before.
2. The adaptation or betterment of an existing product.

Many times we develop a new product that changes the way we do something—such as the Roomba robotic cleaners or Amazon's Alexa that can keep records, help with household chores, compose emails or texts, and in general do things that we never thought possible.

Certainly, in the field of medicine new products and drugs have been invented that have very nearly wiped out certain diseases. Remember, when the x-ray was first developed, we were overwhelmed with its possibilities. That was followed by ultrasound equipment, the CT scan, and now 4D ultrasounds that have opened up a whole new approach for looking inside our bodies. We might get used to one product revolution, only to find that research can improve it even more—beyond our expectations.

Many years ago the Friden calculator, about the size of a breadbox, was used in accounting departments. It was great and we thought it could do all kinds of math, but in reality it could only add, subtract, multiply and divide. Today we have phones that we can hold in one hand, and these do everything in one app that the old Friden did, plus more.

The level of people's desire sets the initial stage for the development of a marketing and customer service program. That initial stage is filled with excitement. However, many new ideas fail due to a poor marketing program or subsequent lack of follow-thru in getting the product to the customer.

In some cases, the product perceived has been so good that it needs little or no service, such as Maytag washing machines. The manufacturer developed that image through very clever advertising. On the other hand, there are businesses whose success is created by the future need. For instance, pharmacists not only sell prescriptions but also provide refills and give advice on the drug restrictions and use, thereby adding to their value.

How New Products Develop Other New Products

Sometimes new ideas, like microwave ovens, can create a whole new line of products. Foods that once could only be heated in ovens can now be prepared more efficiently with less energy. Companies began designing foods specifically for these ovens. Therefore, the development of the microwave oven opened up another new world of product offerings never thought of before.

The Impact of Competition on Product Development

The most successful companies, like Proctor and Gamble, devote a large percentage of their dollars to research and product development, which is always influenced by competition. Whether it's a new idea or cultivation of an existing product that fulfills a need, the competition factor is necessarily in the picture.

These companies are constantly surveying consumers, looking for new markets and making determinations about their current products' positioning. In some cases, even companies like P&G miss the market or misjudge their position. This was the case with "pump toothpaste." The competition came out with this idea before P&G, but it wasn't until these other companies began to take some market share that P&G introduced its own version of pump toothpaste.

The Impact of Competition on Warranties

One automotive company created a program to solve a major customer problem: the "five-year or 50,000 mile" service warranty. Until then, most people had deplorable experiences servicing their car at one time or another. So, because the basic idea of better quality had pizazz, it took the market by storm. Now almost everyone offers some type of extended warranty. Some, of course, are better than "five-years/50,000 miles," but the idea has a double-pronged thrust:

a) The consumer feels that if the manufacturer is willing to guarantee free repairs, the product must be that good; and

b) The consumer knows that if something does go wrong, it can and will be fixed.

How Closely Should You Follow a Competitor?

In some cases, a policy of blindly following a competitor can be unsatisfactory. As an example, the low interest rate loans that automotive manufacturers initially helped increase sale—at first. Once everyone started to do the same thing, it was not a competitive advantage anymore. This new idea gave a push on sales for that moment, but the manufacturers felt the slump afterwards. The idea became the standard, and eventually a new competitive strategy was need.

What to Learn From a Competitor

According to the Wall Street Journal, as of 1987, General Motors reported depressed sales, so they minimized inventory, slashed production and laid off workers. For almost two years prior, General Motors had stubbornly kept nearly all factories humming and tried to keep up its market penetration. The article mentioned that its competitors were among their chief skeptics.

Many believed that General Motor's products, even the freshest offerings, were failing to excite American consumers in the way that the products of those same competitors were—such as Ford's rounded Taurus and Sable mid-size cars and Chrysler's fast-selling mini-vans. In this case, the competitors were right.

The basic principle behind this example stands today. The problem happened again for General Motors in the early 2000s and has occurred for other automotive manufacturers—for example, Isuzu stopped making consumer SUVs in the United States in 2004 because it could not compete with other automotive manufacturers in this area. Fluid response to market demand and honest evaluation of your products in relation to your competition is vital to remaining solvent.

A Service Idea That Promotes Sales

Some retailers did not accept American Express credit cards because it cost two to three percentages more for the retailers to process through their bank, but the service idea offered by American Express of doubling a manufacturer's warranty if a customer purchased the product using their American Express changed that. The extended warranty program created demand by consumers for retailers to accept the card so the consumer would receive an increased warranty even if the retailer were to go out of business. It stimulated retailers to promote American Express, gave the consumer added protection and encouraged sales. The service provided by American Express ultimately provided a fantastic competitive edge to them, helping both American Express and their customer—the retailer. This is the perfect example of where a retailer's policy of not accepting a particular credit card could hurt their actual sales income, but give the retailer who does accept the card a sales edge.

Surviving the Competition

There are some cases, like Ritz Crackers or Ivory Soap, where the product never changes despite their competition. The key is that the product is great and the quality has never changed. Ritz Crackers taste good, are unusual and fulfill a need. Ivory soap works and it never changes. The original sales pitch was true, and the need for a good solid soap has not changed.

These two products dominated the market enough to survive the competition. They also monitored their product performance and stayed on a course that continued to work. But, you should never count on that. Typically, to survive the competition—and beat it if you can—you must be on the lookout for new product ideas, new variations on old product ideas and better ways to serve your customers.

Checkpoint Quiz:

- How savvy is my R&D?
- Do I have a completely new idea for a product that has never been used by my customer base?
- Am I adapting an existing product based on customer need and demand?
- Is my product still the best in the marketplace?
- Am I prepared to upgrade my product or remove it based on an accurate market evaluation?

HOW IMPORTANT IS LOCATION?

Competition may point the way for the ideal location to set up your business. If a leading fast food company starts on one corner, for example, then you can be sure that another will pop up nearby. In some cases, like auto dealerships, this turns out to be a pretty good idea, since customers will begin to identify a certain area as the place to buy a car or eat fast food.

In the case of fast food restaurants, new competition might reduce the number of customers that patronize the first operator. However, if the market is growing and the first store gives super customer service, it can hold its position. Unfortunately, at times the first operator at a location may get overly confident and not treat their customers properly. Once the new company arrives on the scene, customers march over to the new business. If you come in as the new competition and have properly shopped the market, you may see this problem exists. If so, you should go overboard in making sure that you give faster and better service. Even if your food (or your car brand, or any other product) is pretty much the same as the competition's—not better—you will still win, as your service will shine by comparison. This is a case where you don't even need a superior product to beat your competition.

Picking the Right Spot

When you set up a location near a competitor, you should make sure that you study in detail how your competitor's location works, and how they handle customers. Can you drive in easily? Is parking convenient? When you leave, can you reenter traffic? How does the competition inventory merchandise? What about the ambience, the warmth of the people and, of course, the quality and prices? Try to pick out a particular area where your competition is weak and emphasize the contrast in your own.

Let's face it, not every spot is the same, even in the same location. Your job is to promote the features of your site that beat your competition. Some businesses have found that strip shopping centers have an advantage over large malls. Others find malls to be better. Some people find that being on the outskirts or in the suburbs is better than being downtown. Whatever you choose, use it to the very best advantage. Remember to "accentuate the positive" and make your location a plus against competition.

Less-Than-Ideal Locations

Some people claim that business success is determined by "location, location, location." Yet, some stores or restaurants are successful in hard-to-find areas or with impossible parking. So, there really isn't a fool-proof guideline. A competitor's location can either help or hurt you. Your sales strategy can be developed depending on this situation. Even if your competitor has a better location, you can beat him by de-emphasizing location and building up your customer service. That's always a big plus.

Checkpoint Quiz:

- Are you moving to a location near your competitors? Has anyone new moved into your area?
- Have you compared your competitors' strengths and weaknesses to your own?

WHAT FIRST-CLASS CUSTOMER SERVICE CAN MEAN

When the Boeing Company calls its Director of Service Engineering part of "customer service," you realize how unique and important they know their customers are. In order to compete in the big-league airplane market, they have to make sure that their planes continue to fly with an almost unlimited life (the average lifespan of their planes is about 30 years). This means that taking good care of their planes and their customers are Boeing's highest priorities, contributing to their unique place in the market. Leroy A. Keith, once in charge of aircraft certification for the Federal Aviation Administration regional office in Seattle, said, "One reason they [Boeing] have such a remarkable sales record is they take very good care of their customers." Service is a major element in the company's success.

In Cincinnati, Ohio, there was an auto dealer with a similar philosophy who advertised its owner's name and his title, which was "Owner *and* Service Manager." There was no question that service was a major concern for their dealership.

Expect the Unexpected

An industry can often develop a new product that adversely affects a product from another industry. Romantic paperback books were one of the most dramatic demonstrations of a changing market in the past. When television and movie producers came out with "love story" television episodes or films, it threatened the book market, and publishing companies had to find a way to offset such competition. Over the years, people began watching movies and TV instead of reading books. However, since avid readers never completely disappeared, the two industries began to work together. In the early 2000s, it became common for popular books to be adapted to the screen – think *The Lord of the Rings, Harry Potter* and Nicholas Sparks' books. Today, it is common for books that become New York Times Bestsellers to be adapted into movies and vice-versa. The original *Star Wars* movie trilogy was later turned into a book series.

It is vital to be aware that unexpected industry changes or inventions may occur at any time and threaten your organization's success, so you need to remain fluid in a rapidly changing marketplace. Otherwise, your competitors may take advantage of *your* company's weaknesses.

Each Competitor is Unique

No two competitors are alike, even those with the same product. Competitor "A" will always be different from Competitor "B." Therefore, your major job is to determine the differences and use the information for your benefit. Even if you have all the pieces of the puzzle put together, the information often changes, so stay on top of it.

Example: How does a consumer choose between two gas stations? Both sell gas, maybe for the same price. What makes them different, and why would a customer go to one rather than the other? Here are some potential reasons:

- One is easier to enter and leave.
- One will give a customer the same price if they use a credit card—the other will charge extra.
- One offers a car wash (or offers cheaper prices for the wash).
- One will provide road advice for traveling to specific locations if you need help—the other "couldn't care less."
- One has people who always smile, make you feel welcome and say "thank you" for the business.

Since these factors can change weekly, or even daily, you must reevaluate your program and your competitor's program periodically. It might be extra work for you, but these are the kinds of things that make a difference.

Letting Customers Know What to Expect

In the hotel business, there are many policies that need to be interpreted and administered on a daily basis, for example, changes by the banquet department for a dinner or dance. Everything can be adjusted, depending on the size of the function and what is being served. Decorations, flowers, audio visual equipment, the type of service, etc., are all variables. Depending on when the function takes place or with whom the customer speaks, there may different expressions of the hotel's policy. This next tip is important for any organization:

Unless you and all of your people are concerned with maintaining a specific level of customer service, there will be inconsistencies.

The trick is to capitalize on a good, consistent policy throughout your company and to find out where the competition is inconsistent. Consumers feel comfortable when they know what to expect, and they are more comfortable when you respect and adjust to their needs. If your competitors are inconsistent, this can be a useful sales tool for you. It can bring customers to you when they are looking for something better.

It's important to adjust the present situation to your customer. Sure, you have policies, but adjustments within a policy can and should be made within reason. For example, in my hotel business, no dinner, luncheon or meeting was ever the same from customer to customer. Your ability to customize shows your level of "customer service," which your competitor may not do.

Here are two examples of a strong, consistent customer service policy that well illustrates the difference between what should happen vs. what is most common:

The Doctor Experience
a) The front desk answers calls promptly.
b) They determine the sense of urgency for each situation and address the patient's problems.
c) They make an appointment to meet as quickly as possible, according to the patient's needs.

d) The patient receives a reminder call the day before, making sure they know the date, time and location of the office. They are willing and able to give them directions.

e) They make sure that patients are properly greeted and are comfortable in the waiting room.

f) If a wait is more than 30 minutes, they explain the situation to the patient and ask if they want a drink.

g) If the wait reaches one hour, they apologize again and explain what is going on.

h) After the patient is seen, the next appointment is scheduled.

i) If the patient had a long wait, they further apologize for inconvenience.

j) They write the next appointment on a card and give it to the patient.

k) When the patient calls for any reason, they make sure they are called back instantly, and their situation is promptly handled (preferably within an hour).

The Restaurant Experience

a) Remember, it is "opening night" **every day** in a restaurant.

b) If a guest calls for a reservation and their desired time is unavailable, suggested alternate times as close to their desired reservation should be offered.

c) Guests should be called the day of the reservation to confirm.

d) When the guest arrives, the host/hostess should be properly groomed, smiling and welcome them graciously.

e) If a guest doesn't have a reservation, their name should be added to the list and then direct them to a waiting area.

f) If the wait for a table is delayed a long time, the host/hostess should reassure the guest that they are on the list, apologize and consider offering them a complimentary beverage.

g) If guests linger too long after dessert, in order to turn the tables, the host/hostess could offer them a drink at the bar.

h) Once the guest is seated, make sure the server attends to them quickly, offering water, bread and butter, and taking their order.

i) The server should make sure every order is properly taken by repeating it.

j) When the food arrives, the server should know exactly what each person ordered.

k) The server should make sure each guest has the required special utensils, if necessary.

l) The server should visit the table five minutes later to make sure that everything is okay.

m) The server might non-intrusively observe the dining experience, and when guests are finished make sure the table is quickly bussed.

n) After a table is bussed, the server should immediately ask for drink orders and for an item like coffee, bring cream and sugar without asking.

o) The server should take dessert orders and make sure proper utensils are at the table anticipating the delivery of the dessert.

p) Once dinner is finished, the server should thank the customer for being at the restaurant and assume they had a good dining experienced without asking "How was your dinner?"

q) When the guest leaves the restaurant, the host/hostess should thank them for their visit and give them a card about the restaurant so they can make another reservation.

Checkpoint Quiz:

- How can I better monitor potential disruptors in my industry, and, specifically, my organization?
- How often do policies tend to change in my industry? Based on this information, how often do I need to look at my competition and reevaluate my products/services to make sure I can do better than my competition?
- Based on complaints against my company, does every employee have the same standard of customer service? Does our policy need to be more consistent?
- Are my organization's policies clearly stated so that my clients know what to expect?
- How can I improve my organization's ability to customize service depending on the client?

THE IMPORTANCE OF MANNERS
IN A TECH-SAVVY WORLD

One of the easiest but most overlooked ways to turn a negative situation into a positive situation is using these three words: "please" and "thank you." This might seem obvious, but when was the last time you heard someone say these words in a professional or personal conversation?

One of the problems with technology today is that we have gotten used to doing most correspondence by email or even text message, and in these forms of communication we tend to forego that "personal touch," forgetting to use please and thank you. Because of this, we are developing into a society that appears to ignore the niceties of working with other people. We all want to have a good relationship with those with whom we work, and we don't want to appear dictatorial or demeaning to other colleagues.

Saying Please and Thank You

So, what is the secret to success? We have to realize the truth in what our parents have been telling us since birth: "please" and "thank you" are the magic words! Please and thank you are vital to good relationships and good communication in any organization. And good manners are contagious!

Example: Think about when you're driving your car in bumper-to-bumper traffic and another car turns their blinker on to show they want to come into your lane. What might happen if you actually let them in? They may just signal "thank you" and realize that there are actually some nice people left in the world. They might even do the same for the next person!

We all like to work with people who appreciate us and who appreciate working with us. Imagine if you gave someone a gift and they did not say thank you. That would demonstrate their lack of understanding good manners, and it would make you uncomfortable and reluctant to give them another gift.

Those with authority over other human beings have the choice of ignoring manners and being impolite to the employees working underneath them. They might not realize that this will upset their employees, who in turn will pass this disrespectful conduct on to other employees—and even customers, creating a bad atmosphere in the organization. To ensure this does not happen, every encounter you have—whether face-to-face, voice or electronic—should be warm and friendly. This will permeate the organization with positivity.

It's possible in any organization that nobody will want to work with or be inspired by the appointed leader. That's why there is appointed and un-appointed leadership. Anyone in any position can inspire and contribute to the personality of the organization, even if they aren't an appointed leader. If you're a good leader, people will follow you because of your relationship with them and the respect you give them. However, you want all of your managers to be good leaders, and this starts at the top with you.

Giving Your Organization the "Personal Touch"

When I was in the manufacturing business, our company made metal doors and frames. As part of our sales program, we developed a unique way to cut and weld metal door frames into custom units and cut holes into the doors for various types of locks. We also had a training school for our customers' employees, and several times a year they would come to our plant for two to three days of training. When these mechanics came in, I always made it a priority as president of the company to meet and have dinner with them at least once during their stay. This "personal touch" helped develop loyal relationships between the customers' employees and us.

As you can see, what we were really doing was "training" our customers' employees to promote our company, its people and its products. We took time with these people to show them that we *did* make a better product; and, since we spent time with them, they became informal salespeople for our company. They had a chance to see our employees in action, and they were able to see that we were sincere about helping them.

Personalize Your Sales and Service

The key to this program was, of course, the personal touch. We tried to make each "student" feel important. Having dinner with them and spending time with them was positive proof that that we were indeed sincere. When I went around the country to visit my customers, it was always fun to walk into the shop areas and have their workers yell out, "Hi Bob!" We would catch up, and it felt good that our friendships were flourishing.

In the same vein, you should always introduce guests and potential customers to various members of your staff, from your hourly workers to the top-ranking executives. They all make up the company and its personality.

In addition, if a visitor asks any employee about your basic customer policy, make sure your employee will emphasize "good customer service." If you make this a top priority, very few competitors will be able to stand up to the test. In my businesses, I meant it when I emphasized customer service, as did all of my employees, and that policy really paid off. Good customer service may be stimulated by the fact that your competitors don't provide it, but it should be driven first by an obsession on the part of every member of your organization.

Example: I tried a fun experiment with some of my employees when we were trying to pitch a potential customer. This particular company routinely brought a lot of people into town. Our sales manager was worried about our competition, and we felt that we had to do something special. We invited the customer to the hotel, and the sales manager and I had coffee in a suite with the company's representative. At a good opening point in the conversation, I mentioned that all of our staff were interested in earning their business and that we were very "people-oriented." Then, the door opened and in walked six of our department managers, including a few who were factory workers. They each gave a one-minute speech on what they did and why they wanted this customer to do business with us. The customer never saw this before and was impressed—and we got the order. After receiving it, we wrote a thank you letter to the customer and those six people signed it. We were able to demonstrate our "people-izing."

Communication between two people, whether electronic or face-to-face, should have an amicable, comfortable ambiance. People will develop lasting impressions of each other's character no matter the method of communication, and it will be much better if they develop a good impression of you through your polite manners and the use of please and thank you. However, you will probably have to make more of a conscious effort when communicating through email or text, because the other party won't be able to see you or hear you, and they will develop their impression of you based on the words you choose. If you choose your words well, you will develop long-standing and worthwhile relationships.

If you present your organization in a way where niceties are the norm, even in electronic communication, it will be contagious and heartwarming, making for a good work environment. This trickles down to customers, because they'll sense it and feel good that they chose to work with you. Also, since good manners are contagious, you'll inspire others to use them as well, because those who do not have good manners will be noticeably out of place in your organization.

Give Individual Attention to Individual Customers

Giving and receiving the "personal touch" is something very specific to an individual. Maybe it is a hotel owner loaning a customer his car to get to a meeting they are late for. I made postcards with photos of me doing silly things around my hotel because I wanted my guests to know the hotel had a personal touch. Show them how you will address their needs and how you will adjust your product or service to help them.

The overall idea is that customer service does not only matter when you handle a transaction but also in the way you deal with your company and set its atmosphere. Customers can tell when employees do not want to be helpful. There are certain organizations and companies that don't follow an automatic routine of service, but instead personalize each experience—and you can tell that they really care about the customer.

Therefore, customer service is necessary in all aspects of human relationships. It isn't just about having someone provide a product or service; it's about the relationship you have with people. Therefore, customer service is a broad expression for interpersonal relationships and you should always work to improve them.

Checkpoint Quiz:

- Do I use please and thank you when I speak to colleagues and customers?
- Are those under my authority happy and warm?
- If not, how can I set a better example and improve my company's atmosphere?
- How can I encourage my customers to sell for me?
- Where can I add/improve a personal touch to my clients' experience?
- How can I increase my obsession over customer service?
- How can I encourage my employees/colleagues to obsess over good customer service as much as I do?

REMEMBERING THAT CUSTOMERS ARE PEOPLE

In managing my own enterprise, the key operational word (courtesy of Tom Peters and Robert H. Waterman, Jr., who wrote the book *In Search of Excellence*) was <u>obsession</u>. My employees, from executive vice president down the line, considered me obsessed with customer relations—precisely the impression I wished to convey.

Caring obsessively about customers and treating them as people who have feelings is what helps organizations flourish. It also helps maintain a level of excitement in our everyday dealings.

As a manager, I was all for the healthy and profit-stimulating environment in which key executives felt free to call the shots as they saw them, whether they coincided with the chief's viewpoint or not. I respected and encouraged any member of my team who saw my proposed program or idea as impractical to tell me to my face. Therefore, if they didn't realize that the care and handling of customers was the organization's highest priority, they didn't belong with us.

When any emergency popped up—whether it involved numbers, operations or whatever—if a customer problem or complaint interceded, the customer took precedence. This meant that if any of us were in a meeting or doing another task and a customer-related problem occurred, we stopped and took care of that problem. I felt that as CEO I needed to constantly demonstrate this policy so that even when I was not around my staff knew it was standard policy.

Here is a way to test your own skill in good customer service. Record your own telephone conversation and then play it back and see how you sound. Sometimes it's embarrassing and will enable you to teach yourself how to do better. It can also be good to reassess emails you sent that convey by your responses if you were having a bad day or were poorly informed about a situation.

Two Top Priorities

Business is conducted on two levels. Level one deals with the matters of marketing, finance and statistical analysis. A business person would be a fool to understate the importance of these functions. They're the vital organs of the corporate body—kidneys, lungs, liver and the like. But where would these level one organs be without a strong and healthy beating heart?

Level two involves people: employees, suppliers, the public and the consumers. The most important people, as far as corporate goals and missions are concerned, are the company's customers—what they want, what they need, how they feel, how they react and how you can satisfy their needs. The overriding failure of our economy today is an excessive corporate emphasis on the technical and analytical aspects without including the human and personal ones. Zero in on the company's highest priority—the customer and his or her needs. This by no means implies that technology and cost performances must be slighted, but puts them in the proper place.

The most logical and significant explanation for the breakdown of customer service in the marketplace is what psychiatrists sometimes refer to as the principle of least interest. As we travel down the wage and rank totem pole, employees' stake in the business and what makes it successful and profitable tends to diminish—unless they are stirred and psyched into believing that good customer relations are in their best personal interests and will protect their jobs. Convincing workers, and key employees in particular, must be a top priority of chief executive officers and their closest aides.

There are many ways to convince employees. The following is one method:

Convince Employees to Prioritize Customer Service

1. A company's leader must be believable in his/her personal obsession with the organization's customer service policy.
2. A company's leader must communicate this obsession personally to as many staff members as possible. This includes talking to rank and file employees. The message cannot be diluted though word of mouth. It cannot successfully be told by memo or announcement.

It must be done "eyeball-to-eyeball" with staff directly from the company leader.

3. The company must have policies that are helpful—not punitive.
4. It is essential to constantly remind employees of the importance of customer service, and it might even be necessary to fire those who do not follow the "customer service policy." This is one of the most difficult parts of any business, but if the company leader is serious about the matter, it can and must be accomplished.
5. New employees should be carefully screened to make sure they know the company's customer service policies before they accept the job.

When managers are conscientious and concerned with bottom-line performance, the tendency is to focus on the specialized aspects of the business where concentrated responsibility is centered—accounting, financial, production, data processing and marketing. All too often, when customer problems or complaints "get in the way," they are regarded as an intrusion or annoyance and not given proper attention.

Thus, the chief executive's primary task is to generate continuing awareness of the need for top quality customer orientation in all departments. In my company, for example, I scheduled 20-minute orientation meetings on a monthly basis to stress upon new employees the urgency of superior customer service.

Be Obsessed with Customer Service

- Obsession with service is not a once-in-a-while state of mind; it is now and forever.
- Regardless of how busy you may be, make it a priority to sit down periodically with your key decision makers to convey this message and make sure it isn't forgotten.
- Have "rap sessions" with specific goals of improving customer service.
- Do not delegate this matter. Be the "keeper" and generator of your philosophy.

The "Unnecessary" Letter or Phone Call

One of the most important yet overlooked aspects of a good customer relations policy is the simple courtesy of follow-up contact in serving any account, new or existing. Remember the last time you bought a car, appliance, piece of furniture or computer? Or the last time you stayed at a hotel or resort, or took a cruise or tour? Did you get a follow-up letter, email or phone call thanking you for your business and inquiring about your satisfaction and asking whether you had any problems? I have received such follow-ups on occasion, but they have been few and far between. When I do get a letter like that, it has a stronger impact on me than any slick magazine ad or television commercial that costs hundreds of thousands of dollars. Don't you feel the same way about this personal touch?

Since transactions and relationships are so automatic and impersonal today, when personal contact is made it's so unique that it is more memorable and long-lasting.

Consumer-Consciousness

Do you evaluate your company periodically to see if everyone working for you is consumer-conscious? Does your policy make it easy to maintain that focus?

Great Service
• It's human.
• It's personal.
• You don't forget it.

Example: At one time I had been very concerned about the service that our company received when printing brochures and other literature. While attending a concert, I saw another printer's ad in the program and decided to look into it. The next day, I phoned and asked for their owner or president, but was informed that they were busy at the time. After explaining who I was and telling the employee that my company used a great deal of printed material, I asked for a return call. Guess what? No phone call! Naturally, we never contacted that company again because of our first impression of their customer service policy.

Example: While visiting Chicago, my wife Phyllis and I stopped at the Shelby-Williams booth at a hotel show and inquired about some chairs we were interested in. During our discussion, Manny Steinfeld, the company's president at the time, appeared and suggested we take a look at the chairs in question at his country club. He made arrangements to pick us up the next day, drive us to his club and then take us to the airport in time for our first flight out of Chicago. The next morning, when we met the car he had arranged, who did we see? Manny! He said he was not going with us, but he wanted to be sure we met the car. When we went to his club, he called the club manager to be sure we saw the proper chairs. Obviously, he got the order when we bought the chairs. A few months later, we bought some of the company's stock. Shortly after that, we received a personal note from Manny Steinfeld thanking us for our faith in his company.

The first example is easy to compete with. A lot of business can be won and a lot of competition can be squeezed out just by returning phone calls or emails instantly. If a customer says: "I can't decide today; why don't you call me back in a week," do not wait that long. Find some excuse to call within a few days. Don't let your competition have a chance to sneak in and get the order.

It's amazing when you call back quickly how many times the person will say, "I'm glad you called; I have a question," giving you a chance to provide the answer and get the order.

Look closely at the second example. That's service. It's human. It's personal. You don't forget people who treat you the way Manny Steinfeld treated us. And you don't stop doing business with them.

When Persistence Pays

At my manufacturing company, we made steel products for the government and had to buy component parts from an outside source. We took bids, but had not yet decided on the successful bidder. In fact, we had not even studied the bids when we got a call from one of the bidders. He said he was going to be in our city and asked if he could visit us to discuss his bid. We were not ready to talk with him and advised him we would call him at the proper time. The next day he appeared at our door anyway. He stated that he came to our city to see someone else but that appointment had finished early. He didn't have any place to go before his flight and asked if he could use our lobby to work. Well… after seeing him in the lobby for a couple hours, we said to each other, "Maybe we should study the bids on that job, and as long as this person is here, he could answer any questions we have." Yep! You guessed it, he got the order.

Clever? Yes, of course, but it worked because he was persistent and he knew we had to make a decision soon in order to meet our deadlines. Sometimes the right amount of persistence gets the order, because it gives evidence of good service which beats out the competition.

Customers are real live people! They have the same types of likes and dislikes as you and I do. They are the buyers—the ones who make the decision for their companies. If you want to be successful, then you must be sensitive to them. Your policies, plans and programs must be "people-oriented."

Checkpoint Quiz:

- How can I better demonstrate my obsession for consumers and their concerns?
- What are some ways that I can convince my employees that our consumers are the priority and not an intrusion?
- When can I fit in "rap sessions" to continue to emphasize service to my employees?
- How can I incorporate personal follow-ups with clients into my organization's policy?
- How can we be more persistent in dealing with potential customers?
- How can we be more consumer-conscious?

CUSTOMER SERVICE IN TODAY'S ECONOMY

The current trend in customer service is closely following the current trend of the consumers' attitudes. Courtesy has fallen by the wayside. Road rage is common. Arguing is considered acceptable, but demanding is even more common.

With all the problems we have in getting good service, organizations should give more attention to this subject. The most successful companies are giving good service and are profiting from it. However, some CEOs think that it's automatic: "Sure we give good service; that's our business." But, strong customer service policies are often nonexistent or not enforced by so many.

Recent Trends

Tom Peters, in his book entitled *A Passion for Excellence*[1] says that the care and feeding of the customer is the most dominant part of any business. He further states:

- "...in the words of Rothschild Venture's Arch McGill [formerly the youngest vice president in IBM's history]: 'The individual [customer] perceives service in his or her own terms.'" (I always add to McGill's line: '...in his or her own unique, idiosyncratic, human, emotional, end-of-the-day, irrational, erratic terms.')
- "Surely, it's obvious that everything necessarily starts with the customer. More specifically, with common courtesy toward the customer."
- "...The relationship between the man and the customer, their mutual trust, the importance of reputation, the idea of putting the customer first—always—all these things, if carried out with

real conviction by a company, can make a good deal of difference in its destiny."

- "The perceptions of human beings are all there is. Let's come to grips with all this—it's the essence of managing and marketing. And leading."

The book *Service America*[2] emphasizes that we are now living in an economy where organizations must perform rather than produce, and where physical products are distinguished by the quality of a company's service. It shows how service management can turn a company in any kind of service field into a customer-driven and service-oriented business.

The authors develop the "Moment of Truth" idea—the critical instant in which customers come into contact with the organization and form their impressions of its quality and service. When a customer makes his first personal contact with an employee, this Moment of Truth becomes the time when all your sales efforts, training of employees and best opportunities to develop and keep a customer are utilized. It is the time when you can either "blow it"—or make the kind of impression that is important to your business.

According to John Naisbitt in his book *Megatrends*[3], the years 1956 and 1957 were a turning point and the end of the industrial era of our country. He quoted Harvard sociologist Daniel Bell, who termed the time a "post-industrial society." At this point, the industrial industry was not the dominant part of our economy. We had become more of a service-type economy. "We know," said Naisbitt, "that this period is the information society." He further commented that the number of businesses in service positions had not grown, but a large number of service jobs are not engaged in the creation, processing and distribution of information. "The so-called service sector," he said, "minus the information and knowledge workers has remained a fairly steady 11 or 12 percent since 1950… the real increase has been in information occupations."

The Growing Demand for Better Service

Consumers hesitate in calling the president or CEO of companies they deal with, even when they have serious problems with a product or service. If you have a major legitimate complaint with something, it might be wise to consider calling the president of the company. The heads of companies are more accessible than ever, because you can find this person's email address, Facebook account and phone number easily on your computer or phone. In most cases you'll be surprised by the help they offer when you explain your legitimate concern objectively. You might be able to talk to them about your situation. It's rewarding for you and can be very helpful to the company, since most leaders rarely talk to a customer about real problems. Try it. Then, put this into practice and ask someone to do a random test to see how easily accessible and helpful you are.

Psychologist Elliott Jaffa of Arlington, Virginia, turned timid salesmen into hard-charging, aggressive go-getters at Baltimore Learning Center Open University, a private center for lifestyle courses. Jaffa taught Chupza 101 (his spelling). Tired of waiting in a doctor's office? Jaffa suggested entering treatment area by using the restroom, commandeering an empty treatment room and, when a doctor goes by, saying 'Hi, I'm next.' Doctors may get mad, but they speed up service. At hotels, Jaffa suggested using the hotel chain's name as your middle name. Smile and say, 'Please, no special privileges.' The ploy usually produced complimentary fruit.

Now, I'm not suggesting that we attend a class like "Chupza 101," but we are influenced more and more by customer service or the lack of it. There will be times when we are "stuck" and cannot do much about it, such as at the post office or an airline that serves an area on an almost exclusive basis. But generally, we do have a choice and we are not always influenced by product price alone. This is where a detailed study of the competition is necessary, not only for their quality and price, but for their service and service functions.

The Rule of Service Businesses

In his book, *Managing in the Service Economy*[4], James L. Heskett, professor of Business Administration at Harvard Business School, introduced "strategic service vision." This is a logically organized plan for businesses to implement their ideas, and it focuses on the changing environment in which they manage. Professor Heskett stated "a service cannot be all things to all people. Unlike product manufacturers, service organizations can have considerable difficulty delivering more than one product, more than one type or level of service at one time. Groups or segments of customers must be singled out for a particular service, their needs determined, and a single service concept developed that provides a competitive advantage for the server in the eyes of those to be served."

Filling a Real Need

It may be possible that you—unlike your competitors—can find one or two items in your company's policies that can be improved. For example, my hotel business was able to get a successful account because our competitor did not provide sufficient bellman service. The customer had been using a competitor's meeting rooms with a hotel room as an office. Every morning the customer had to call a bellman to move his equipment from the hotel room to the meeting room. The bellmen were always checking out guests in the mornings, and were often unavailable to this particular customer. When he came to us for prices and information, he told us his "horror story" and asked if we could provide bellman service. We promised, and the day he checked in we gave him his own bellman cart with his name on it to keep in his office. Simple? Yes, but here's a case where the inept policy of the competitor helped us to win a customer. The competitor's mistake had not been a deliberate policy; it was just a matter of inadequate management follow-through. And we benefitted from it.

The smallest annoyances usually cause the biggest problems. Many companies, often to their disadvantage, only concern themselves with the major aspects and ignore the details of better customer service.

In contrast, there is an auto dealer in Texas who will pick you up on the road for free if a car you bought from them ever breaks down. The dealer sells its service department before it sells a car. It wants you to know that when you buy from this dealer, you will be taken care of regardless of what happens to your car.

The Roepnack Company, a building contractor in Pompano Beach, Florida, did something similar. It made follow-ups after its one year guarantee expired. They handled all of the details, completely taking away the worry from customers successfully, until the owner retired.

How Do Customers See Customer Service?

David R. Huhn, former president of McAlpine's Department Store in Cincinnati, Ohio, was quoted in a newspaper article as saying that service is a long-term operation. At the time, he did not wish to give away too many secrets to his competition, but he used such projects as the corps of "mystery shoppers" periodically to check up on things, and his individual stores conducted employee contests to improve service.

In 1987, to more clearly focus on any problems with service, I surveyed about 2,500 hotel customers, providing a good cross-section of the service-buying American public. Completed questionnaires and responses were returned from approximately 10% of those surveyed.

The purpose of the survey was to identify the customers' ideas about service problems in various areas, not just in relation to my hotel. It enabled us to identify areas that needed attention to provide the best possible service to these customers, and to gain insight into the competition to see what they were doing.

The survey touched a raw nerve because almost every respondent added his or her "horror story" of poor service, most of them written out in graphic detail. Many ran on for pages and pages, indicating the depth of bitterness about the cavalier way customers were treated:

> "Recently, I was in a department store and walked over all of the store to find a cashier. I stood in line. Finally when it was my turn, the employee told me to go somewhere else – it was her break time. I said I had walked all over the store, there were no other cashiers, and I was the only one left in line. I was told that it was my problem and she left for her break. Did I make a purchase? What do you think?"

> "I guess the worst is when you go to an expensive store, hotel or restaurant and the employee feels either that you don't have enough money (because you are dressed in your scruffy clothes) or you can't afford something there. They automatically pass judgment without knowing that you might just be the wealthiest person in the world. Each customer should be treated with the same courtesy."

"My car was damaged by an elderly man who suffered a stroke and lost control of his car. His liability insurance refused to pay my damages because his stroke was 'an act of God,'" and therefore not covered. It took many letters, phone calls and the intervention of the Florida Insurance Commissioner to get my claim covered."

About half of those surveyed said the service they received as customers was downright awful or poor or at best only fair. They reported that customer service had been deteriorating for years. Some thought it would get still worse, while others believed it had bottomed out.

Aside from service from federal and state government offices—which evoked the worst marks from respondents—auto service departments headed the list of those with bad service.

Neighborhood shops, on the other hand, were widely recognized as giving the best service. This was followed by hotels, motels, insurances companies (when selling, not when handling claims) and airlines. Banks also fared well with most of the respondents.

Some of the most common reasons for poor service listed by respondents included:

- Too much employee turnover to build up strong personal customer relations (cited by almost half of the respondents)
- Shortsightedness—the feeling that companies can make money without good customer service (also cited by almost half)
- Service people and owners feeling that customers have no choice but to come to them
- Businesses becoming too big
- Too much absentee management

Despite the bitter feelings revealed by the survey, a surprising 18% of respondents found customer service improving, and about 38% hoped that it will get better in the future.

Some categories were rated "excellent" by some respondents while rated "bad" by others. There were no hard and fast trends, but the survey certainly showed how many people feel. Clearly, customer service is a matter of personal opinion and individual experience. Those categories were:

Excellent service: (in order)	Worst Service: (in order)
• Neighborhood Shops	• Federal and State Government Offices
• Hotels and Motels	• Auto Service Departments
• Insurance Companies (when selling)	• Local Government Offices
• Airlines	• Auto Dealers
• Packaging delivery and moving companies	• Gas Stations
• Supermarkets	• Post Offices
• Restaurants	• Insurance Companies (when handling claims)
• Brokerage Firms	• Department Stores
• Banks	• Doctors' offices
• Doctors' offices	• Banks
• Lawyers, CPAs and other professionals	• Landlords
• Auto Dealers	• Plumbers, Electricians, etc.
• Department Stores	• Airlines
• Post Offices	• Lawyers, CPAs and other professionals
• Plumbers, Electricians, etc.	• Packaging delivery and moving companies
• Insurance Companies (when handling claims)	• Insurance Companies (when selling)
• Auto Service Departments	• Supermarkets
• Landlords	• Restaurants
• Local Government Offices	• Hotels and Motels
• Gas Stations	• Brokerage Firms
• Federal and State Government Offices	• Neighborhood Shops

The respondents were about equally divided on whether the trend toward franchised businesses has had a favorable or unfavorable impact on the quality of service the customer receives. Of those saying franchising made things better, the reasons that got the most votes included:

- Better management training
- Better management controls
- Better employee training

- Stronger, more direct competition
- Better employee motivation

The respondents were asked what action, if any, they themselves take when they are subjected to a serious breakdown in customer service. Most claimed to be activists, as indicated by this ranked order of responses noted:

- Stop doing business with the offender
- Ask to talk to the boss
- Spread the word to others about the poor service
- File a formal complaint with the company
- Demand better service
- Notify the Better Business Bureau
- Contact a government agency
- Shrug it off philosophically

The questionnaire asked: "When you are the recipient of good customer service, do you express your thanks with a verbal pat on the back, a letter to the person's boss, filling out a comment card, or other appropriate action?"

About half said they always do; about a quarter said they occasionally do; and the rest admitted they rarely or never do.

Then came the real zinger: "Being totally honest, how good a job do you think you and your own company do in providing customer service?"

About half said they personally do an excellent job, and the other half settled for just doing a good job. Of all those surveyed, only five rated themselves as just fair, and nobody gave themselves a poor or awful rating.

The respondents didn't give their own organizations quite such glowing marks as they gave themselves personally, but the rankings were still quite high. About a quarter rated their organizations as excellent, half gave a grade of good, fewer than one in five described their organization's customer service as only fair, and only three of the total number of respondents gave their places a poor rating. One lonely respondent said he thought his own company's personal service to customers was awful.

Despite practically breaking their arms to pat themselves on the back, more than three out of four of the respondents said their own companies could improve their success if they put more emphasis on customer service.

There was further evidence of these trends. The National Better Business Bureau in Washington, D.C. said—at the time—that of all complaints reported to the Bureau, 23% were the result of bad or unsatisfactory service. Another 32% were about delivery delays, damage and unsatisfactory repairs. Can you imagine 55% of complaints received by the Better Business Bureau from around the country being service related?

Checkpoint Quiz:

- What core strategy comes from Tom Peter's quote, that "the perceptions of human beings are all there is" in your organization?
- How does your company handle the "Moment of Truth," developed by Carl Albrecht and Ron Zemke?
- What is your organization's policy for handling a customer with Chutzpah?
- If a customer tells you a horror story, can you think outside the box and create a sale?

USE TODAY'S CUSTOMER SERVICE
TO GET NEW CUSTOMERS

In order to find out how things were going nationally now, I decided to contact the council of Better Business Bureaus. This organization coordinates data from all the Better Business Bureaus around the country. I was interested in getting some statistics and information on how they feel about the status of customer service in our country. After several months, I was finally able to get some information from them (I guess they were very busy), and to my surprise they gave me improved statistics on customer service. Apparently, there are about 875,000 complaints nationally that are recorded by the council, and in 2012, 14% of these complaints were about customer service. However, in 2016, only 8% of those complaints were about customer service. The council was happy to report that I might be overly concerned about the problem of bad service, since their statistics showed they are getting less complaints.

After thinking about this data, I discovered that several factors affect the BBB and their customer service complaints. First of all, statistics show that online shopping sales have almost doubled in the last few years, representing over 15-20% of retail sales. When people buy online, the transaction is reasonably accurate—there is usually no personal contact and generally a lot less complaints. In addition to this, instead of using the old-fashioned "call the BBB," customers find that social media offers tremendous possibilities in vocalizing complaints. In some cases, these complaints are handled almost immediately, because the organization in question does not want millions of people to see this complaint on Facebook, Twitter or other social media platforms. So, although the BBB shows that they are getting a lot less complaints, it doesn't mean that consumers are less concerned. It would seem to me that the BBB has a problem that I'm sure they are addressing in the fast-moving retail business.

It's very interesting to see major changes in the ways in which we buy goods and services and receive delivery of those goods and services in unique ways. I still think that we have a problem with providing good service, but it is being recorded and identified in different ways now. It also seems like the complaints can be addressed more quickly, which is very exciting. As we know, comments that are placed on the internet never go away and are always a reminder for companies to do a better job—and perhaps they may even be recalled in the future by the company to show customers how quickly they responded and were able to correct situations. This is a new form of customer service!

In some cases, a product is purchased online and found to be ineffective or not fulfilling its purpose. In one case, someone ordered a protein powder online and the use of it made them sick. The person notified the company online and an apology email came instantly, and in the mail the company delivered a gift to apologize for the problem. This shows how social media can be used, not only to hear about problems, but solve them and satisfy more customers. The world of technology can be used to customers' advantages to make purchasing goods and services easier and more effective.

Service Complaints Can Affect an Entire Industry

In 2017, United Airlines made a drastic error in customer service. They removed a doctor from a plane against his wishes after the plane was loaded, injured the doctor and caused confusion for the flight—and the world learned about their terrible customer service. It's amazing how one improperly handled instant can cause such calamity in a company.

So many social media platforms blew up in reaction, causing the airline tremendous financial loss, a great decline in the value of their stock and reason to think about making major changes in their operations. It forced the company to quickly make changes in the way in which they operated the boarding of their planes. Because of the adverse publicity on social media, other airlines also reevaluated their procedures. It's interesting that in today's electronic world, one instant on one airline on one flight can be heard around the world and cause changes to the entire industry.

In a smaller way, restaurants, doctors, lawyers and retailers can have their services exposed through social media, too. This is quite a change from the way in which we provided these goods and services in the past. I think that companies and organizations now recognize that their service or delivery of goods is more transparent than ever before. Even lawyers and doctors who treat their clients improperly find themselves more rapidly exposed and adversely affected.

Providing good customer service has become even more important now that it can be so easily exposed if it's done improperly. The reaction can be instant and broadcast to millions of people in an instant. WOW! At the writing of this book I am 92 years old, so I find it mind-bogglingly dramatic and hope it will become the stimulus needed to improve customer service.

You can use examples of the United Airlines of your industry to help lure a customer away from a competitor. How? By providing instantaneous, solution-oriented customer service through all media platforms to lure customers from you competition, as well as good customer service on-site.

Luring Your Competitors' Customers Away

This may seem easier said than done. Yet, many astute business executives are carefully and methodically finding these dissatisfied customers and doing their best to steal them away from their competitors. When a customer is dissatisfied or unhappy, that customer is in the mood to "get even." Catching customers in that mood, of course, gives you a good chance to "sell" them. This can be a bit tricky because there still may be loyalties to the other guy; and, you have to do things that are far superior in order to win someone over. You have to convince the customer that what you are doing is the standard procedure for all customers. If you don't do that, they may feel that you are being condescending or taking others for granted.

One of the best ways to find out if you are in the process of stealing a customer is to have a policy of always asking customers how they became aware of your business. To this, a customer might respond: "Oh, I used to buy from XYZ, but they did this and that, so I thought I might try you." This process has additional benefits, since it enables you to see whether customers pay attention to your ads.

Where Are New Customers Coming From?

It never hurts to try to find the source of business. Are customers finding you by word of mouth, through social media or by advertising promotions? Many times this provides a clue as to what you are doing right or wrong in your promotions. Obviously, word of mouth is great because it means that your customers are becoming salespeople for you. This type of "third party" endorsement is, of course, always the best.

Holding on to a New Customer

When a competitor's customers give you a chance, it's time to really show your stuff and impress them with your service. Is this the first time they have patronized you? Where did they shop before? With proper questioning, you can obtain a lot of information. Then, make sure your staff knows what to do with this information.

As former *Businessweek* Editor-in-chief Lew Young states: "In too many companies, the customer has become a nuisance whose unpredictable behavior damages carefully made strategic plans." Don't let that happen to you.

Competition determines sales policies in progressive companies. A sales policy should be in writing for the public to read and executed properly by your staff for the benefit of the customer. For example, you cannot run a cash-only store if your ticket item is high and if your competition gives terms and takes credit. Nor can you have a policy of aiming for customer satisfaction and then argue with a customer.

Competitors' Sales Policies

The Publix grocery chain has a sales policy of carrying your groceries to your car. It works well and is very pleasant. Their main competitor, Winn Dixie, does not do this. Here, then, is a case where a competitor does not follow a rival in the same market.

In this case, Winn Dixie holds its own in the marketplace by advertising, promoting itself as the "meat people," and having very competitive prices. Also, the chain has been very smart in picking good locations. In some cases, the stores get business by the mere fact that they are close by. In other words, they do not worry about the "carry out" policy of Publix – they ignore it! Winn Dixie also developed a better seafood department. All in all, it really becomes a matter of personal preference as to the layout in the store, people, location and your own experience whether you shop at either Publix or Winn Dixie. The prices are about the same in both stores and they both have sales from time to time. The nearby Publix has an organic Greenwise marketplace, whereas the nearby Winn-Dixie has a kosher section. Each has a slight edge on the other.

What Surveys Can Tell You

Marketing surveys provide a glimpse into public opinion and buying habits. However, these exercises are only as good as the people taking part in the surveys; and, you can't be positive that you'll get accurate comments from the consumer.

For example, a consumer might say that price is a significant element in the consumer product buying decision. On the other hand, if a product comes on the market with some unique feature, it is possible that the consumers will disregard their basic cost feelings and, through impulse, buy the higher-priced product. Sometimes packaging, new elements of the product and fashion are features that trigger the buy, even though price is usually an important feature in selecting that product.

When Price Matters Very Little

A perfect example of this is in the apparel business. Blue jeans can be purchased for as low as $10, or upwards of $1000 for designer jeans at exclusive shops. They are both jeans having some style and probably wear similarly. Therefore, what makes the buyer make the decision of one over the other? Obviously, both types of stores sell jeans and, therefore, the buy-in depends on how consumers feel. Do they want status and image with the designer label? Or are they really looking for just "a pair of serviceable jeans?"

This is also a rare example of where the quality, or even the existence of customer service may not apply, since the customer has determined in advance to buy one product or the other. In the example, it is unlikely that the person buying the more costly jeans would be paying designer prices just to go to a store with super service.

This example of price range is somewhat extreme, of course. In most cases the price deferential is not quite this large and, therefore, the comparative prices may be easier to disregard.

Example: If I go to an auto dealer to purchase a car that costs $10,000 from Dealer A and then go to Dealer B, whose car may be bought for $9,800, I might pay the extra $200 for Dealer A's auto if certain features were present:

1. Closer to my home.
2. Highly recommended by friends and neighbors.
3. Dealer A's service and attitude toward me as a customer were more impressive.

On the other hand, if I were to go through this same exercise in the purchase of five cars for my company, the $200 difference becomes $1,000 and, therefore, more significant in my buying decision. The higher-priced dealer would have to sell his organization to me in a more persuasive way, and I would have to be convinced that I would save this money in the long run with the better service and better attention to my fleet of five cars. Fortunately, in our economy we do not always decide on price alone. We are, as consumers, influenced by salesmanship, desire, style, convenience, long-range savings and service. The trick is for the seller to convince the buyer that he is making the right decision in any case.

A well-run company, which is operated by a CEO obsessed with service, will sell more goods and services on that philosophy in the long run than the company that does not provide good service or only sells on price. My son, Jim, for example, owned and operated three ComputerLand stores in Cincinnati. He didn't sell a product at the lowest possible selling price. Yet, he had been highly successful. His customers knew that he and his company provided the utmost in customer service and follow-up after the sale was made. My other son, John, worked in the hotel business, and he was also obsessed with service. It would sound like a tape recording to hear him talk and take action. All three of us are strong believers that good customer service is desirable—and profitable.

Checkpoint Quiz:

- Do you use social media to respond to customer complaints?
- Do your employees ask new customers what brought them to you, and do they know what to do with that information?
- What do your competitors do differently? Does it matter?
- Is price the final answer?

A SERVICE-MINDED TEAM

Having your competition hire all of your ineffective employees would probably be one of the best sales moves you could make for your own company. But you shouldn't have any people like that in your company anyway. Nothing is worse than working hard to develop a product or service, bringing the customer to your door, and then blowing it with a poor sales presentation.

Of all the areas we have talked about, it would seem that your ability to know about your competitor's salespeople and how inferior they may certainly be is an area in which to "beat your competition." Most salespeople are products of the management of their company. As was mentioned before, they reflect in their actions the real policies and personalities of those companies. Once again, take advantage of this in establishing your company's personality.

When your team "feels" the company's policies—especially when it comes to service—they can better communicate it to customers. In other words, instead of doing the typical "play acting," each member will be honest and sincere with a customer. This sincerity will come through and demonstrate the point. You cannot play games with good customer service and give it only once in a while. Your staff must know it's a basic policy and an expected function! Many of your competitors probably either do not think this way or do not spend enough time getting this across to their salespeople.

The Salesperson as "Service Rep"

Here is a real chance for you! If your local competitor is a large centralized company whose local management changes often, you can show your company's personal touch via your own individual attention. The salesperson is the major link between your company and the customer and must be service-minded—just as the bank teller is the link between you and your bank. If the teller is courteous and helpful, that's apt to be your impression of the bank as a whole.

Good salespeople are able to present their products and services accurately and understand how to adapt the services or products to fill the customers' needs. This is a "people-to-people" exchange, and if a salesperson is properly trained, the customer will feel the true warmth and character of the company.

It is hard to believe that with so many consumers experiencing terrible service, very few are doing anything about it. In most cases, the salesperson had a chance to correct the problem or prevent it but didn't do so. If you ask, customers are usually happy to share their favorite horror stories about the poor customer service which they have encountered from someone. Even doctors, lawyers, accountants and bankers may provide lousy service, forgetting that their patients or clients are also their customers.

The Psychology of Service

It is strange that so many of us demand service although, on the flip side, we tend not to offer service when we have the opportunity.

We must battle customer service insensitivity on two fronts: the corporate front and the academic front. Since academia is the preliminary training ground for executives-to-be, it is here that customer service must be espoused and the danger of ignoring it made clear. On the corporate front, virtually every successful and outstanding company is customer-sensitized, and invariably headed by a chief executive literally driven on the subject of providing exceptional customer service – and having salespeople with the same outlook.

Beginning Service Orientation Early

If there ever was a time for the corporate and academic communities to join forces, that time is now. America has long been a world leader in technology, and business schools have been at the forefront of innumerable breakthroughs. However, what is still missing is understanding the customers' concerns and feelings and how competition can affect a business. Academia has fallen sadly behind in teaching how to probe and accurately read customers and how to respond to their needs and desires in simple human terms. Not only have our schools fallen behind, they have failed to recognize the importance of cultivating good interpersonal relationships. Because of this, our business leaders may not have the ability to train their team in these personal skills.

H.J. Zoffer, former dean of the University of Pittsburgh's graduate school of business, an educator aware of the problem, states the case bluntly enough: "We need a way to reach the spirit, develop the verb and create the need for venturing to light the fire of creativity in our students so they understand the difference between administering and managing."

Bravo! A painful reality to confront is that too many graduate and undergraduate school professors live in the cocoons of university life, from which they rarely emerge. Dean Zoffer views this as a "compounding problem," that the "growing cadre of obsolescent faculty who need their functional expertise repositioned for a management world changing too fast to accommodate their yellowed notes."

The time is long past due for business people and the teaching profession to combine their resolves, minds and resources. Urgently needed are more advisory councils and interchange programs in which hands-on managers trade ideas with professors. Such a restructuring and readdressing of the elements of success in the marketplace would greatly enhance corporate bottom-line results, fill more college classrooms and lecture halls, and, most importantly, cause countless customers to cheer.

In order to find out more about this from first-hand experience, I wrote to approximately 50 deans from schools of business asking about customer service and trying to collect data on their attitudes:

- "As stipulated previously, there is not enough time in the program or room in the curriculum to fit everything, including customer service. In other words, trade-offs must be made, both conceptually and pragmatically."
- "It does not enjoy a definitive taxonomy; that is, should personal or impersonal services be addressed? Does the discussion focus on firms primarily engaged in services (dry cleaners) or firms which manufacture products and uses the services attribute to differentiate themselves in the competitive arena (e.g., IBM?)."
- "More emphasis is being channeled toward 'customer service' as witnessed by additional chapters in marketing text devoted solely

to service: textbooks per se focusing on service marketing; and increase in seminars concentrating on customer service, the firm's competitive edge."

I believe a real breakthrough will occur. At Lynn University, I worked with former dean Ron Usiewicz to develop and put into effect a college credit course on customer service in the hospitality curriculum. This was probably the first time that an accredited college had taken a gigantic step in business education. This course covered the real live world of customer service. We collected books on the subject and even developed "live experiments" that students had to perform.

In their own interests, all business people should try to provide themselves with some sort of educational tie-in with business education. Options include:

- Junior Achievement, a high school program that teaches high school students how to organize and run a business.
- Teaching a class on certain areas of business to a study group, small business group, or a tech school or college.
- Business co-op programs for school and work, available in both high school and college.
- Membership in business advisory boards at schools and universities in their area.

Business Leaders as Teachers

Having a businessperson partake in some part of the educational process can go a long way in promoting good solid business training for up-and-coming business people. This, in turn, translates into doing a better job of training staff to promote good customer relations.

An enthusiastic businessperson can do wonders in inspiring the value and excitement of a company. It is contagious and it is rewarding to see the results. There is also a good by-product in this exercise: the businessperson learns a lot from the experience. He or she can profit from the questions raised by students and probe his or her own mind for the answers. When a businessperson finds he must defend and analyze his decision in a classroom with students, he may develop a different outlook.

We may not normally think that competition has much to do with the subject of sales training, but it does in a couple of key ways. First, the degree of training we give our staff in using our competitive edge is important. It is one thing for the management to develop programs to beat competition, but it's another to be sure your employees execute it in a proper way. Making sure that your employees are equally concerned with providing customer service—better than the competition—is very important.

> - How does the salesperson handle the customer who says he is going to buy from your competitor?
> - How do you fight this?
> - What will the salesperson do?

With proper training and knowledge, the salesperson can have meaningful answers, point out flaws in competitors' proposals, and play up the merits of their own. The salesperson who is properly trained can, of course, fight the competition more quickly and more skillfully. Time may be the determining factor, with the salesperson having to make quick decisions and know what action to take. In some cases, if the salesperson is able to call the home office or headquarters on the spot from the customer's place of business, he or she can put on a good show for the customer's benefit. The salesperson can tell his or her boss in front of the customer what has to be done and how crucial it is to either meet the competition's offer or make certain concessions or promises to impress the customer. The salesperson can demonstrate authority and underscore the importance of the customer to the seller.

The Competitions' Training

Another aspect of training is evaluating the flip side. How well are your competitors' staffs trained? Many times your competitors' salespeople can almost "work for you," since their lack of knowledge, training and efficiency can highlight your people's ability. This breaks down customer confidence in your competition and builds a good image for you. Knowledge of your competitor's sales staff, then, can be critical to your strategy.

If your own sales staff is active and on the ball, you will probably come into contact with your competitors' salespeople. When this happens, you can usually learn the goals, attitudes and policy of your competition. For example, my vice president of sales once went out of town on what is called a sales blitz for our area. We were greatly helped when our competitors' salesperson wasn't as active and didn't do well at presentations. Our vice president was able to shine in comparison and discover their weaknesses.

Another way to evaluate a competitive salesperson is to see what he or she tells a prospective customer. In other words, what was the pitch? Did the salesperson impress the potential customer or not? Having a link to the academic world and being comfortable in a training mode will make it easier for you to judge these things and to find and keep salespeople. Your competition may be very weak in this area, leaving it up to you to take advantage of this opportunity. Certainly, listening to sincere employees speak with great respect about their boss and the company—after hearing something different—is a pleasant experience to most customers. Your competition will not be able to catch up to you if you have this type of organization.

To sum up, your own sales organization and the training your people have in promoting your customer service policy are the best tools to fight competition. Many competitors drop the ball in sales training; they only teach product knowledge. You can offset that by teaching your people the value of strong customer service. In the past, a few people left my company to work for the competition. It's always interesting to run into them and hear their horror stories about their "new company." If they do this, they probably aren't sincere when talking to customers. It made me glad they were not with us any longer—it showed their poor judgment in complaining about their new company.

Checkpoint Quiz:

- Is your team a product of your company's management style? Do you approve?
- What is your company's service policy?
- Does your team convey the warmth and character of your company?

- Do you have an educational tie-in? Do members of your team have one?
- If there is a horror story in your company, is it easily shared and corrected without reproach?

BECOMING MORE CUSTOMER-CONSCIOUS

In establishing a sales policy, it is customary for companies to create a plan and detail every mechanical and administrative issue, including:

a) How a product will be distributed.
b) The various price levels in terms of sale.
c) The unit and packaging of a product.
d) The repair or replacement policy.

Very seldom is much thought given to sales policies from the customer's point of view. Jacobson's, a former specialty store located in various cities from Michigan to Florida, had a printed policy as follows:

Jacobson's Courtesy

We believe courtesy and caring are as important as beautiful merchandise. Dependability, integrity, personal attention and satisfaction are priority considerations at Jacobson's. Pleasing you is the total concern of our entire staff.

Jacobson's Service

Doing something extra for you is a matter of policy at Jacobson's. We will help you plan a wedding. Register your bridal or baby gift preferences for the convenience of family and friends. Gift wrap and mail a package at your request. Validate your parking ticket. Do your personal shopping for you when you are rushed for time or undecided in a gift choice.

Personal experience showed their stores not only stated these policies but they actually carried them out. After making many purchases one year, my wife found that she was overloaded with parcels, when all of a sudden a sales employee said, "Let me help you carry the parcels to your car." How many times have you had this happen to you? Naturally, we became great supporters and regular customers of Jacobson's during their heyday.

Spreading the Word

According to a study made by research firm Technical Assistance Research Programs, Inc. (TARP), consumers who were completely satisfied with the service told an average of four to five people, and consumers who were dissatisfied told nine to ten people. Word of mouth communications show the importance of developing a sales strategy to beat your competition.

In a working paper report published in 1983[5], TARP concluded that "companies work very hard to develop good products and service and to attract new customers. During product delivery, however, the customers' real needs are forgotten. Marketing can fall in love with its own 'hype' and Operations implement standards which are easy to conceptualize, measure and fulfill. Unfortunately, customers are more interested in their needs and their unfulfilled expectations translate into lost revenue and higher after sale costs."

What Sales Policies Really Mean

In order to use your competition as an aid in selling your own service, make sure you can learn what the competitor's real policy is – not just its printed or spoken word. What does the competitor do in actual situations? You can "shop" the sales policy simply by being a customer and by talking to other customers. Look for policies that are weak or that may not be carried out. Here, again, you can use what you learned to your benefit, by emphasizing that customers can trust in you. Gordon F. Shea, President of the Prime Systems Company, said in an AMA Management Brief [6] that "a sound organization, like a sound person, has invested time and effort in building a reputation people can trust." He further said, "The confidence of others often makes the difference between success and failure."

The problem is that many sales policies are only theories and are often misinterpreted or improperly carried out by others. A financial executive, for example, may establish certain terms and conditions that are not competitive. Since a company cannot change the market, its policy should be altered to address the needs of the market. When you make these discoveries, it's a great chance to enhance your own image and improve your standing with customers.

Wording Your Policy the Right Way

Many sales policies are unwritten, which makes "shopping the policy" so important in strengthening your position against your competition. Sales policies should not be punitive toward the customers, such as "YOU must have your sales slip on returns," or "YOU must return in two days or else." Instead, they should be worded in a positive vein like: "We accept returns and if you have the sales slip, it will expedite the process," or "If you are dissatisfied, you may bring it back. If you cannot do this within two days, please call us to discuss how we may help you in this matter."

The owner, the CEO or other person making the decision must realize the impact of a good policy—properly stated—on the customer. Then, when the policy is established, it must be implemented by the boss. Don't delegate it. Remember that a positive customer-oriented sales policy is a good tool in selling effectively and beating the competition. Develop it, train your staff in its use, implement it, and finally, monitor it regularly to see to it that it is always in place and working.

Checkpoint Quiz:

- Is your sales policy written from the customers' point-of-view?
- Does your company fall in love with its own marketing hype?
- Do you "shop" your competitors?
- Does your team convey your sales and service policies the way you think they should?

HOW SALES JUDGMENT ATTRACTS AND HOLDS CUSTOMERS

One of the most exciting marketing adventures in business is the strategy planning required to land a new customer or to hold onto an old one. In both cases, competition is the driving force that directs your judgment and guides your thoughts in order to accomplish your goals.

The most difficult part of devising this plan is to be sure to have all the facts. Do you really know what you are up against? Do you know what the customer wants? Are you sure that you know what factors will influence the decision?

Do you know with whom you are competing? Do you know the right decision maker? In order to get all of this information, top executives often depend upon others to provide it. This is where they may have trouble in sorting out "hearsay" from actual "facts." Your personal business judgment is required in order to determine that you have the right data for the decision process.

Sales Judgment in Action

My brother and I were in the manufacturing business, making building products and selling them all over the country. We heard that one of our largest customers was thinking about changing to buy from a competitor. So we studied, gathered the facts and made our plans. We visited the customer with our sales team, and put on a sales presentation as if the customer was not already ours, but only a potential customer. We really went all out and when we were finished with our "pitch," the customer thanked us and said, "OK. You got it; we're your customer. You have reconfirmed our thoughts. You have reassured us that the competition is not as good as you. We really were interested in seeing what you would do! And you didn't disappoint us."

Our judgment in this case was right. The presentation was a lot of work and very expensive, but it taught us a good lesson: Your competition is always at your customers' doorsteps. You cannot let down your guard. The art of keeping customers is as important as that of getting them. The judgment factor of what to do and when is the critical element in such a marketing scenario.

Good sales and marketing executives who have brought their companies to the summit of success are always alert to competition and to timing. They are motivated by the movement (or lack of it) in the competition. And, they exercise the skill and judgment necessary to "win the game."

Checkpoint Quiz:

- What do you do to land a new customer?
- What do you do to hold on to them?

MEETING THE COMPETITION

Very seldom do you hear a sales strategy that says "Our goal should be to make our customers successful." When I was with Steelcraft, we took a chance by keeping it a single product-type company. We made metal doors and frames, and that was it. We felt that we had developed the best product with the best quality, although probably one with the highest selling price. Our success was due in part to the way in which we built up our distribution network, our customer base. When we got a customer, they stayed with us and the customer developed a loyalty that was almost unparalleled. Our key was to make the customer successful in their own business. We demonstrated this almost every day and our customers knew it by experience.

Playing on Your Customers' Self-Interest

Once my firm had a sales meeting in Florida for our customers. About 500 people attended and we paid for most of the event. It was a huge gathering–expensive, but worthwhile. The meeting was built around the theme of "How to do a Better Job in Your Business," and we hired experts in various fields to speak and educate the participants. But these experts dealt with subjects pertaining to the customers' businesses. Prior to the meeting, our experts had visited some of our customers and learned their problems. The presentations were about these problems. It was not theoretical or "up in the air," but to the point. We even had our lawyer discuss wills, passing your business on to your kids, etc. Everyone was waiting for the company pitch on our own products—but we never did it! We kept the meeting as promised, and though expensive, it was a definite statement of our loyalty to our customers and our commitment to their success. We certainly were ahead of our competition, and no one, we felt, could ever copy this idea.

Acquiring Information about Competitors

Most businesses know very little of their competitors or their customers, certainly not the way Steelcraft did. Much of their information is incorrect, and may be embellished by the salesperson to either enhance a point or to be an excuse for not getting business. One of the most important things to do is to figure out the best way to acquire information about your competitor. Here are a few suggestions:

1. Call or email the competitor and act like a customer. Ask questions. This will usually produce some information, though not enough. For top results, you will usually do better in person, but general data can be secured through a phone call or email.
2. Have a friend shop the competition and actually buy their product or service and report to you. Make sure the facts are accurate.
3. Have a professional shopper get the best non-emotional facts. Incidentally, this is a good idea to use on your own sales team to see how they are really performing.
4. For out-of-town competition, subscribe to the local paper in that city and save any articles about them. This is easier, of course, when the competition is located in a small town.
5. Create a questionnaire for your sales team to use with customers who say they use the competition. See if you can derive some accurate data about why.
6. Watch your competitors' ads and read their literature carefully to make sure you understand in detail how their products or services stand up to yours.
7. If you're in a type of business where you can visit the competition's establishment, then do so. Take pictures or get first-hand information. It's amazing how much information employees give out about their companies.

The study of competition takes all kinds of direction and discipline. You do not just sit down one day and say, "Let's study our competition." You may never uncover all your rivals. For example, in the hotel business there is competition for rooms, in addition to our meeting, convention or banquet facilities. These might include:

a) other hotels, motels or resort hotels
b) people who rent their condos or homes to vacationers
c) golf and tennis clubs, country clubs and boat clubs that offer rooms
d) meeting and convention facilities
e) country clubs
f) church halls
g) service club halls
h) restaurants
i) all of the above in other cities, both domestic and foreign

Responding to the Competition

Your competition is not always so visible. For example, one company rented many of our rooms. At one point, we discovered that a condo was being used to house some of their people staying over a long period of time. As it happened, the company person assigned to make the rooming deal was a relatively new employee, having moved from another city. Before his family arrived, he was put into one of these condos. When he related his distaste over these arrangements, we naturally "accentuated the positive," taking advantage of a competitive situation for our benefit. This was a good lesson for our entire sales department.

Another example of "invisible competition" comes from the laundry and dry cleaning business. Through technical advances, "wash and wear" clothes and other materials that were developed hurt the dry cleaning business in a serious way. Their competition was not the store next door, but rather technology itself. Look what disposable diapers did to the diaper business!

Beware of First Impressions

When you're faced with a competitive threat, analyze the situation carefully to determine the specific competition in that area. What are the best attractions and worst features? Relate those to your particular facility. Be sure that you obtain factual information on the competitor's policies, prices and offerings. Even then there may be doubts as to the full picture because of unknown details about the competitor's people—its staff and their relationship to their customers.

The Right Sales Tools

For example, ever since deregulation, airlines have been using price as a sales tool. Before that, only routes, service and cities serviced were the sales tools. Today with deregulation, it's a "no holds barred" game in the industry. It now seems as if the best tool the airlines have is price. Airlines also used "frequent flyer" campaigns to award customers with free flights on their planes after a certain number of miles traveled. This type of program was so successful that the hotel industry joined in with similar programs. The point is that in the airline business—as well as in the other—it's no longer easy to determine what gives the competitive edge. It's difficult to determine why a customer uses one or another airline or other service. You have to examine all the possibilities.

What Strategy is Right for You?

When good, accurate information is secured about a competitor you can more accurately establish a solid sales strategy. As previously stated, you should be sure that your sales policy is not established by sales management only. Delivery, inventory, floor planning, terms, packaging and completeness of line are all items that can affect sales and edge out competition. Since there are items controlled by different executives in a company, this means that everyone should be involved in setting sales policies. Meeting the competition is not just the sales department's job; it takes coordination and a deep understanding of the customers' needs. Don't let the finance department, for example, kill a sale by some unrealistic demands on terms of sale. Be relentless in your accurate knowledge of the competition, because it constantly changes.

Checkpoint Quiz:

- Do you know how to make your customers successful in their own business?
- How many different types of rivals compete for your customers?
- What is your invisible competition?
- Can the decisions of any department in your company cause you to lose a customer?

WORLDWIDE COMPETITION AND HOW IT CAN AFFECT YOU

Our country's history demonstrates a policy of past isolationism. For a wide range for reasons, we felt it was unnecessary to aggressively pursue foreign markets. On the other hand, many foreign countries have recognized our market and profitably expanded into our "turf" (so to speak). Consider the following observation:

"Global competition and horrendous U.S. trade deficits would seem to dictate more and better American efforts overseas. Is this happening? Nearly 100 executives at U.S. companies with at least one foreign subsidiary agreed to this logic in a poll by Egon Zehnder International, the world wide executive search firm. But agreement doesn't mean action. Two-thirds admitted that U.S. managers were woefully ignorant about foreign markets; and nearly two-thirds said few of their top executives had significant international experience. What's more, efforts to look beyond the water's edge rated little encouragement."

The above quote from *Forbes*, December 20, 1987 issue[7], under the "Trends" section, stated the problem very well. It means we must consider foreign competition just as much as American competition and try to understand the thinking processes behind them. It means that foreign competitors may have different goals and ambitions for their companies and products. Also, since many foreign governments subsidize their companies, it means the true cost of their products is not borne by the market. It may be hard for us to understand a mentality and culture so different from our own. Yet, in the same issue of *Forbes*, we read: "Max Jamiesson, formerly a top executive with Toyota's U.S. Sales arm, made it clear that Hyundai, the Korean car maker, plans to do precisely what the Japanese did: break in at the cheap end of the market, then infiltrate the more profitable middle of the market."

The Attempt to Beat Us at Our Own Game

This strategy is not new, but illustrates the seriousness of foreign competitors and their determination to beat us at our own game. They realize the need to have the right distribution set-up. American consumers have been willing to accept less service from them because the initial selling price of imported products was so low. When the same type of service was provided by importers that the American car makers gave, it meant double-trouble for American businesses. This dictates some good solid rethinking of our customer service policies.

In many foreign countries, businesses are willing to forego instant profits and put more money and time into research and development. In America, our companies are urged by investors to go for quick profits, and while we spend huge amounts on research and development, it is sometimes held up to provide more instant profits. In some cases, our foreign competitors set the tone for innovative and unique product development. However, an outstanding example of just the reverse is the Motorola Two-Way Radio. Motorola was able to compete in the Japanese market and enjoyed a good sales volume of its product in Japan before they brought their products to market on U.S. soil.

Long-Term Goals

Years ago, we only had to worry about competition from our own cities, states or country. But now our sales and customer service policies are, in some cases, set by companies in other parts of the world. Occasionally, we are caught unaware of new products that could make ours obsolete. Look what happened to the 16mm movie camera business, which had a nice market for cameras, screens, film and related accessories. Along came the camcorder, a video tape camera that used an inexpensive tape in color and was easily be shown on a VCR. Now people prefer the ease of their smartphones and tablets for both pictures and movies, although there is still a smaller professional market for the specialized equipment.

This whole situation means that American business people must become worldlier and more understanding of what other countries are doing. Our customer service thinking must encompass this world market. Business isolationism is a thing of the past.

American Products Abroad

If you travel around the world you will see the impact of some of our American products: Coca-Cola and other soft drinks, fast-food franchises, autos, magazines, computers, medical devices and medicine, to name a few. All of these items, in one way or another, compete with the products of that country or satisfy a need in that country. With the introduction of McDonald's in Japan, hamburgers became a delicious new concept, certainly taking business away from typical Japanese restaurants. This is an example of how a new product (new to that country) can impact the economy and actually change the habits of some of the population.

Years ago, Mainland China had very few entrepreneurs in the country – it was forbidden. All business in China was officially government-owned and operated. There was generally an area in most towns where they did permit some private business to be conducted. I was amazed that the few people acting as entrepreneurs were really hustling their goods. One had a pig for sale, another sold some ice cream and one even sold pepper. It seems that the entrepreneurial spirit is practically born in some since, obviously, they had no chance to train or study.

On this same trip, I visited a trade fair and was able to see products that they were making in China for the world market. Some of the products were really "early vintage" versions of ours. Yet, to some countries where these products are sold, they would be considered by the buyers as state-of-the-art, since they don't know any better. The buyers in a third world market may be less sophisticated or less knowledgeable or simply glad to find any new product that will solve a basic problem in their country. However, as buyers in third world countries became more knowledgeable of what America and other developed countries were doing, they made technology a key factor in any purchase requirement if possible.

What's Ahead?

The world, through communications and transportation, is becoming smaller and the exchange of information is greater. This means that product and service technology is all over the world and that competition has become worldwide for most products and even some services.

Checkpoint Quiz:

- Is there foreign competition in your market? Is there a foreign market that's right for your company?
- Is your company R&D-driven or profit-driven? Is this the right place for you to be?

THE FUTURE OF COMPETITION

There are many factors to consider when evaluating the future. Your competition may change from a competitive company to new product developments, obsolescence and changing needs. For example, we thought of hospitals in traditional terms: doctors sent patients who stayed as long as they needed. As the population grew, there were more patients.

Unexpected Obsolescence

What happened? New medical developments meant we could cure people faster. Instead of a week in the hospital to have a baby, for example, the stay is currently two or three days. In addition, quick med-centers and urgent care facilities provide "out-patient" care at a lower cost. Instead of going to traditional hospitals for tests, these centers refer patients to facilities owned by them or connected to them in some manner for further tests.

New Kinds of Competition

Doctors are "wined and dined" in the hope that they will use certain hospitals; and in some cases, hospitals help doctors begin their practice. Since a doctor is really a kind of salesperson for a hospital, it's important for a hospital to have on its staff as many good ones as possible. "Good" means not only those who are the best technically trained, but also the ones that would admit the most patients: doctors who are ear, nose, and throat specialists or internists or surgeons. So, many hospitals began to compete for doctors' attention. The old timers already had connections with hospitals. Therefore, it was necessary to have new doctors develop loyal ties with the hospitals. Hospitals began to realize that they, too, have to run a business, and with it face the stresses of competition.

They needed to develop a "sales strategy" to connect with more doctors and patients. Hospitals began to run ads and develop new ways to get patients.

Since the government limited fees that hospitals could charge Medicare patients, and hospitals often found they had empty beds, they set up other companies to provide lab or x-ray services to supplement their income. The result was that the entire industry changed, and what was once thought of as a forever situation is now completely different. The hospitals that forecast those changes were able to move with them, and they survived. Others sold out to large companies or merged with others. All of this happened in spite of good customer service even when they were able to keep pace with their competition. What will the future bring to this industry? Probably continued new treatment in faster periods of time and smaller hospitals with money-making labs that also do research on non-medical items. The hospital will become science labs in addition to a place for healing people.

New Demands to Be Met

We are living in a world of high technology. The world, through communications and transportation, has become smaller, and the ability to exchange information is always expanding. We think the changes revolutionizing all of the industries are unique, but they probably aren't as unique as we think. I think the steam engine and the television were considered a dramatic change in their respective times, but there have been so many new technologies and changes since then. What is incredible now is the rapid increase of the speed at which these changes are occurring. What will my great-grandchildren be living with when they come of age? When I first saw the comics with Dick Tracey, who had a radio wristwatch, I said to myself, "Gosh, this would be something really unique if it was real." Never did I envision that it would become an everyday item that could do so much more!

Changes occurred throughout centuries and continue to occur now. For example, you may think it is normal, but retail has undergone a tremendous revolution – not only the ease and ability to purchase goods online, but also in the many other ways people can purchase goods and services. You can use Apple Pay almost anywhere, you can tell Amazon's Alexa to purchase something for you, and you can get "buttons" that you press to reorder certain products like Tide detergent and Bounty paper towels.

Reading glasses are advertised on television today, which you were previously only able to buy at an optometrist's office. However, because of this, individual attention as part of the process of buying goods and services is becoming increasingly less common. Therefore, the way in which people handle customer service is changing as well, because technology changed how consumers handle problems with services or products purchased.

New developments provide consumers with automatic services and trouble-free products. Packaging of goods will make products more convenient, and manufacturers will have to be ready to move quickly to keep up. Voice-activated computers, remote-controlled appliances, service-free products and automatic testing with easy and replaceable parts are at the forefront because of consumer demand for better service.

You may not have to be first in the market with these innovations, but you have to be better. Sometimes it's wise to let the market develop and then enter with a better product. Your competition then absorbs the great introductory costs and begins to open the market, after which you can emerge as a lower-cost producer with a better product and an attractive selling price.

Most consumers want increasing amounts of service with convenience. With longer predicted life span and increased mobility, we will be able to do more. Obsolescence of products will increase, and businesses that are alert, worldly, flexible and observant will win!

Creative Innovation

Our American economy is born of creative and industrious innovation. We haven't always been alert and flexible enough for the future. Trains were once thought of as just trains and not a future mode of transportation. Steel production was not modernized or maintained with the best technology. We are still making auto engines with the same venerable principles that applied to the first invention. A single outage of a transformer can cause a blackout in several states.

For us to survive, therefore, we must hasten our acceptance of innovation and the need for it. We are still building our homes brick by brick, and many of our needs are fulfilled in traditional ways.

What we must now do is stimulate our thinking to be creative in our market techniques. Instead of just thinking product and product development, we should consider service and customer service orientation. We, as companies, should stand and be leaders in the development of these trends in better customer service. Maybe this will lead us to a product or a product change and an overall obsession with fulfilling the need for better service. This will in itself direct strategy and development for the future. We are going to become so service-oriented that we will be uncomfortable with anything else. Competition, then, will be a follower rather than a leader.

New Needs for Service

This is already happening in the hotel business. As long as you have a clean, contemporary and well-priced hotel and provide the ultimate in personalized customer service, you will get and keep customers. From a marketing standpoint though, what's contemporary changes often. We once focused on the "Yuppie" market, and now at center stage are the "Ultras," people in the 50- to 65-year old category. Their children have "flown the coop," their mortgages are paid off or reduced and they have freedom to enjoy life. Their needs and desires will stimulate business in service-oriented directions that may be different from anything we've known.

Probably the most important trend for the future will be the continuing development of techniques for gathering and processing information. This will continue to categorize companies and products and services. Competition will become even more impersonal, and buying decisions will be made by electronics instead of the personal touch. The personal computer has already made giant strides in every phase of our life, in education, medicine, records and decisions we want to make. Our small children are becoming technology-smart and at such early ages, that as they grow up it is second nature for them.

The Westinghouse Company took a model home in Coral Springs, Florida, and tried to develop the "house of the future" electronically. It was TV controlled with cameras and screens throughout, and electrical devices controlled almost everything. As part of that development, there was a program to shop at a local store electronically. The idea didn't materialize then, but with increased technology innovation, their ideas came to life after all.

New ways to compete and new market products will emerge, offering greater opportunities. Technology not only makes our life better, but with it brings the problems of competing for the consumers' dollar and the need to seek new business in different ways.

Advances in customer service approaches are being demonstrated by certain progressive companies. Michael Jordan, former president of Pepsico, was quoted by *Restaurant & Institutions* magazine, saying: "The home-delivery phenomenon is telling us people want to consume the product in a more convenient fashion." His company, which owns Kentucky Fried Chicken, Taco Bell, and Pizza Hut is very involved in this approach. Mr. Jordan further states, "The whole thrust of his company's food service strategy is to fit the logistics of consumer needs. That's clearly what is behind delivery."[9]

In another article in *Restaurants & Institutions* magazine, Nancy Ross Ryan said: "Competition, a key element in entrepreneurship existed primarily between like subs-segments. Cafeterias would compete with other cafeterias for market share; steakhouses with other steakhouses. Now the boundary lines of competition are beginning to blur as new, trendy, moderately priced restaurants proliferate, offering a viable option to fine dining: twice the fun at half the price."[8]

Some Things Won't Change

When changing with the times and modernizing your business, don't forget you are still dealing with human beings. Automation and modern technology are great, but with all the equipment and electronics, if you forget to smile and offer good customer service, you might as well lock the doors. Customers like the accuracy and speed with which a machine can handle a situation or give an account balance. When a problem occurs, however, everyone hates to be reminded of the computer's capabilities. Everyone becomes more people-conscious. Show your customers that you are willing to take the time and expend the personal energy to be of help. In the survey mentioned earlier, one customer reported:

"I had not received a bill for over six months on a credit card purchase. I called into the credit card company and asked that they bill me so I could clear up the account. Two weeks later I received a "Past Due" notice threatening collection! I sent a letter of complaint and cut up my credit card."

All of us believe that our business system is the best there is, but the impact of competition can offer instant devastation even within this best of all possible systems. The trend to more entrepreneurship means flexibility and this means having the ability to move fast. We all say that competition keeps us on our toes. Yet, when it hits home, we sometimes panic. This can cause confusion, irregular policy and customer dissatisfaction. However, a steady deliberate response to competition, its risks and its benefits, can produce top-quality results.

How to Treat Customer Complaints

- Answer your phones as if you were waiting for that customer's particular call.
- Don't slouch on gallantry and etiquette.
- Don't be a machine.
- Don't let your employees be machines either.
- Machines themselves do not draw customers, but your competitors surely will if you don't give the service the customers want.

Checkpoint Quiz:

- Are you aware of changes in the market that could render any part of your company obsolete? Do you have a plan for that?
- Are there new demands that might create opportunities for you?
- As customers age, can you meet their new needs?
- If your market ages out, what are you doing to reach the next generation?

WHAT CAN BE DONE?

"Students across the country are getting down to business – not to academic endeavors, but to running businesses as diverse as banks, export companies, investment funds, daycare centers, and toy and novelty manufacturers."

This quote, from a *Wall Street Journal* article, shows that teaching children the art of commerce is so vital to our survival. Junior Achievement has long been a successful program in high schools across America. Local business people work with high school students to start a temporary company, run it and try to show a profit. As the *Wall Street Journal* stated, companies are started by students and do not go out of business, but are kept by the school to be run by the next class.

Many business colleges around the country have business advisory boards, consisting of active businesspeople who give guidance and help these colleges. Their programs will help in making our population more aware of the problems of business and the need for it to be successful in our world economy.

Improving the Picture

As high school students are getting into more programs on business, maybe we can tackle another neglected but important part of the educational process for good customer service. The survey of 50 schools of business throughout the country mentioned earlier revealed that none of these schools had any courses or programs specific to customer service. Some of the schools protested that it was "discussed in marketing classes," but others were very interested in the subject, and may give consideration to doing something more in this field. Part of the problem we have is that we are not discussing this enough in our business schools or elsewhere. We are not preparing our business students on proactive and reactive customer service and its potential impact on a company's competitive position. "Customer service" is sometimes only words, and its significance is not widely recognized. It is only when a CEO or business owner becomes obsessed with the idea and uses it to advance his company's standing in the marketplace that customer service is properly implemented.

When You Are a Customer

The real answer to improving customer service and to sharpen competitiveness is for you and me (the consumers) to stand up and be heard! If you don't get good service, don't buy! If you are mistreated, write a letter to the president of the company. After all, you can easily access the information on your phone. If you are upset, make sure the business knows it! And when you are unhappy, tell your friends. The smart competitor will be glad to have you as a customer.

This, in my opinion, is the only way to keep businesses competitive and on their toes. Don't be a complacent customer. Get your service and money's worth on every purchase of goods or service.

A Final Word

Now that we have technology that enables us to transact business globally, talk to each other around the world and shop around the world, the personal attention to our buying needs can disappear. We are not necessarily going to have the interplay of human relations to convince us of one choice or the other.

Customer service, after all, requires a personal touch. And the organizations that take notice of this fact will be able to capitalize on it in a big way. They'll be able to hold on to established customers, attract new ones and gain—and keep—an edge on the competition.

Providing customer service is so simple, inexpensive and obvious. It makes you wonder why we have to preach to organizations to provide it! It is elementary, fundamental and necessary for people to enjoy human experiences. And don't forget that saying simple expressions like please and thank you indicate your personality, respect and other human qualities.

Leaders of organizations should do something now by declaring their obsession in providing respect to their customers. They should not delegate this obsession. They should expand it and preach it.

Remember, it is like enthusiasm—when it is divided, it multiplies.

TEN COMMANDMENTS FOR BEATING THE COMPETITION

1. Keep an absolute *obsession* with high level service. The owner and high-level managers should not only preach customer orientation incessantly, but eat, drink and live it too.
2. Maintain continuous owner and high-level manager visibility. Your top people must meet with your customers.
3. Publicize owner identity. If you are an independent owner, say so and capitalize on it.
4. Work hand-in-hand with customer contact people. When salespeople appear with prospects and customers, greet them personally and voice your feelings about customer service.
5. Give key customers your personal telephone number. Take a cue from top reps in the insurance industry and be accessible.
6. Spread the word. If you are obsessed with customer service, pause to publicize this fact. It will be the pause that refreshes.
7. Make as many personal calls as you can on as many customers as possible – if for no other reason than to thank them personally for their business.
8. Don't screen your telephone calls: calls in general, but customer calls in particular. You will learn a lot more about your business by accepting your calls.
9. Seek opportunities to be of special assistance to customers. Help them if you can.
10. Follow up. Contact new customers as quickly as possible to thank them for their business. Ask all your customers if they have any problems or complaints and invite their ideas and suggestions. Convince them of their continued value to you after the sale.

SIX STEPS TO SUCCESS

You can increase your small organization's potential for success by using the methods discussed below. In addition, use outside advisers, such as your accountant, banker and lawyer to help you over the rough spots.

1. **Cater to customers.**
   - Your number one job should be to please customers. Roll out the red carpet for them. They keep you in business.
   - Learn their likes and make them know you are interested. Give an extra bit of service. People will remember and tell others.
   - Be an expert on your products. Tell the truth about them even if it means a lost sale.
   - Build on existing customers. It is easier to increase their purchases than to draw in new people.
   - Always thank customers.

2. **Build an image.**
   - A small firm needs steady and solid promotion. Part of building an image is using social media, ads, radio or TV spots. They set the stage.
   - Many a store suffers because the owner fumbles his role at the point of sale. Use your personality and manners to encourage people to think favorably of your store and its goods.
   - A clean, well-lit store creates a favorable image of its product.

3. **Encourage teamwork.**
   - The satisfaction customers get from trading with you will only be as good as your employees.
   - So don't keep secrets from your staff. Give them the facts about merchandise. Let them help decide what to put on sale and how to display it.
   - With teamwork, employees do their jobs without prompting. Teach them to know what to do, how to do it, and when to do it.
   - Praise employees in public. Correct them in private.

4. **Plan ahead.**
   - Teamwork makes it easy to plan ahead. Employees who can do a variety of jobs save your time for management work.
   - Watch the calendar for special events which need advance preparation. Look at weather apps as a clue for planning special sales.
   - Train an assistant. Put him in charge and take a day off. This will help him learn.
   - Look ahead. Estimate your sales and cash flow for the next five years. Make plans for financing the store's growth if you don't sell anything.

5. **Look for profit volume.**
   - The name of the game in a store is profit. A big sales volume does not necessarily mean a high profit volume. Profit depends on what is left after you pay your bills.
   - Keep expenses in line. Make a list of both fixed and variable expenses. Rent is an example of a fixed expense; you have to pay it even if you don't sell anything. Bags and wrapping paper are examples of expenses that vary with sales.
   - Determine your break-even point—the point at which sales volume and expenses are equal—and use it as a control tool. Your sales volume should be way beyond the point at which your revenue and expenses balance.

6. **Pay your civic rent.**
    - A store's opportunities for expansion are tied up with the growth of the community in which it is located. When a city has a reputation for being a good place to live, it is more apt to hold residents and attract new ones.
    - You pay your civic rent when you take part in local clubs and other organizations that work to build the community.
    - One caution: Take on only what you can handle. It is better to use your management skills effectively on a few projects than to squander them on many.

FOOTNOTES

1) Peters, T.K., & Austin, N.J. (1985). *A passion for excellence.* New York: Random House, Inc.
2) Albrecht, K., & Zemke, R. (1985). *Service america.* Irwin, Illinois: Dow Jones.
3) Naisbitt, J. (1982). *Megatrends.* New York: Warner Books, Inc.
4) Heskitt, J.L. (1986). *Managing in the Service Economy.* Boston: Harvard Business School Press.
5) TARP (1983). *The bottom-line implications of unmet customer expectations and how to measure them.*
6) Shea, G.F. (1984). *Building Trust in the Workplace.* New York: American Management Association.
7) Trends. (1986, December 20). *Forbes.*
8) Ryan, N.R. (1987). Takeout and home delivery. *Restaurants and Institutions.*
9) Jordan, M. (1987, January 7). *Restaurant and Institutions.*

ACKNOWLEDGEMENTS

My thanks to Desiree McKim and her daughter Tegan for their research, guidance and help in preparing this book and helping me to accomplish this goal of this publication. I wrote this book as a member of the Silent Generation at the peak of my career in the 1980s. In updating it, I collaborated with Desiree, who is from the Baby Boomer generation, who has had successful careers in numerous fields over 37 years, and Tegan, a member of Generation Z who is already successful, preparing to graduate with her MBA at 21, and who formed her own tutoring company at 16, as soon as she entered college, tutoring university-age students. My thanks to them.